Table of Contents

Fiction

Short Stories
The kids in these stories get into their own kind of trouble. How will they get out?

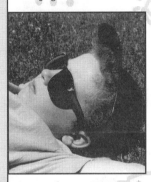

Myths and Folktales
Why does suffering exist? What must an underdog do to triumph? These are the questions answered by the following tales.

Poetry

Poets play with words and ideas to create interesting pictures. Read these poems and join in the fun!

Table of Contents

Information

Nonfiction gives you the facts you need to understand a subject or get a job done.

Biography
Other people's achievements show what you might accomplish.

Making Sense

FICTION · POETRY · INFORMATIONAL READING

Red

Senior Editor	Terry Ofner
Project Editors	Pegi Bevins
	Cecelia Munzenmaier
	Shawn Simmons
Permissions/Research	Cynthia M. Martin
Intern	Anna L. Hemberger
Art Director	Randy Messer
Designer	Jan M. Michalson
Reviewers	Penny Beers, Ed.D.
	English and Reading Program Planner
	School District of Palm Beach County
	West Palm Beach, Florida
	Charles J. Shields
	English Department Chairman
	Homewood-Flossmore High School
	Flossmore, Illinois
	Robin Willis
	Reading Specialist
	Riverside Indian School
	Anakarko, Oklahoma

© 1998 Perfection Learning Corporation
1000 North Second Avenue, P.O. Box 500, Logan, Iowa 51546-1099

ISBN 0-7891-2332-0
Printed in the U.S.A.

Table of Contents

Information cont.

Science and Technology
Test the scientific thinking of these authors.

Social Studies
Interviews, maps, and tomb paintings bring the past to life.

BECOMING AN ACTIVE READER

Active readers don't just read—they interact with what they read. Active readers focus their attention on what they are reading and use strategies like the ones below.

Active Reading Strategies

- **Ask questions**—Active readers question anything they wonder about or don't understand. For example, if an active reader reads that the main character is going to "go a-courtin'," that reader might ask "I wonder what you do when you go a-courtin'?" An active reader would then be on the lookout for clues that would answer that question.

- **Make predictions**—Active readers predict what might happen based on the information in the story. An active reader who is reading a survival story, for example, might predict that the characters will miss a chance at being rescued.

- **Clarify**—Active readers look for answers to their questions and predictions. Once their questions and predictions are clarified, active readers gain a better understanding of the text.

- **Make connections**—Active readers relate what they are reading to their own knowledge and experience. For example,

an active reader who is reading about a dog might compare that animal to a favorite pet.

- **Evaluate**—Active readers draw conclusions about what they have read. By evaluating a selection, active readers are able to form their own opinions about characters, actions, and the selection as a whole.

- **Determine the meanings of new words**—Active readers try to figure out what new words mean. They may look in a dictionary, examine the different parts of the word, or read the surrounding text for clues.

- **React personally**—Active readers comment on different aspects of the text according to their own beliefs and attitudes. An active reader might decide that a certain character is selfish or generous, based on the reader's personal feelings.

A good way to understand a selection is to combine the **Active Reading Strategies** with the **Think-Along** method. Readers who "think along" jot down their thoughts as they read. An example of the Think-Along method is provided on the next page. Look in the right-hand column to see what one student was thinking as she read "Anansi Falls Into His Own Trap." What questions or comments would you add to the Think-Along?

ANANSI FALLS INTO HIS OWN TRAP

An African American folktale
by David Haynes

Think-Along

Anansi, as you know, was usually a clever one, but sometimes he was too clever for his own good.

One time he lived in a kingdom where there was a magical queen. She was a kind ruler, but one thing made her crazy. It seems she had a secret name that she could not bear to hear. Because when she did hear it, she became enraged and did foolish things. So naturally, she forbade anyone to say her secret name. If someone did, she'd cast a spell with her magic powers. This incantation caused the speaker to drop over dead on the spot.

An **incantation** must be the same as a spell because it causes the speaker to die. (**Determining the meaning of a new word**)

But clever Anansi discovered the queen's secret name— *Five.* And that wasn't all. Then he cooked up a plan to get himself an easy meal any time he wished. Here's how he did it.

He pulled his favorite marbles from his bag and wandered down to the water's edge where he knew that many of the animals came daily for a cool drink.

What's he going to do with marbles? (**Asking a question**)

"Excuse me," he said to the mouse. "It seems I've forgotten my glasses. Can you tell me how many marbles I've got here?"

"Well, let's see," said the mouse, trying to be neighborly and helpful. "I see one, two, three, four, five!" And with that, the unfortunate mouse keeled over dead. Anansi made a quick and delicious meal of him right there.

So that's what Anansi is up to! (**Clarifying the answer to a question**)
That Anansi is really sneaky! (**Reacting personally**)

Next, along came a poor chickadee. Also a kind soul, she found herself victim of the same scam. Unsuspectingly, she became Anansi's midmorning snack.

Things went on this way for awhile. Anansi grew big and fat. He continued to eat his way through each day. But, as always happens, word about Anansi's scam got around.

This should be interesting. (**Reacting personally**)

One sunny afternoon, Sister Guinea Hen—who was just as clever as our friend—wandered to the water's edge. There she discovered old Anansi lying back on the beach with a toothpick dangling from his greasy lips.

"Who goes there?" he cried, his voice dripping with helplessness.

Anansi reminds me of the wolf in "Little Red Riding Hood" (**Making connections**)

"It is only me, Brother Anansi," cried Sister Guinea Hen. "Look at the lovely eggs you've laid on the beach!" With that, she ran and sat on a shiny, blue marble that was swirled with streaks of red and white.

"Ha!" Anansi laughed. "The old girl is as blind as I pretend to be," he said to himself. "I'll show her a thing or two!"

"Good to see you this fine afternoon," he said. "Can you help me with something? It seems I've misplaced my glasses, and I'm wondering whether you can tell me how many of my marbles remain." And he licked his lips in preparation for a tasty afternoon snack.

"With pleasure!" exclaimed the guinea hen. "I see one, two, three, four, and . . ."—she drew out the count for maximum effect—"and the one I am sitting on." With that, she perched herself on top of the fifth egg.

Anansi was speechless with shock. Here he had prepared for another meal, and he was faced with a stupid woman who could not even count. "Could you do that again, please? I think there must be some mistake."

"Of course," replied the hen. "Let's see. There is one, two, three, four, and then the one I am sitting on."

"Aargh!" cried Anansi. "Where did you learn to count? This is not even close to being right. Once again, you fool."

Sister Guinea Hen rose up and stood beside the eggs. "One, two, three, four, and this one here," she said, in a perplexed voice.

Anansi seethed and sucked in through his teeth. "I am losing patience with you. How many is that? How many are here?"

"I don't understand," cried Sister Guinea Hen. "What do you mean?"

"I want to know how many," screamed Anansi. "You counted yourself and there are five!"

In his rage, he had said *five*, and of course he fell over dead. Sister Guinea Hen plucked him up and had a delicious meal. She hobbled on back to the village, happy and full.

As for playing this trick on others, well, that didn't happen with this wise old bird. She had seen firsthand what comes from being too greedy.

Sister Guinea Hen better be careful. **(Reacting personally)**

Sister Guinea Hen is pretty clever. **(Reacting personally)**
Maybe she is the one who outsmarts Anansi. **(Making a prediction)**

I was right! **(Clarifying a prediction)**

The lesson here is that if you take more than you're entitled to, you might be sorry. **(Evaluating)**
I'd say that's a good lesson for today's society. **(Reacting personally)**

Reading Fiction

Reading a story is like putting on a pair of glasses. Authors create lenses through which we can see their world. These lenses are most obvious when two authors write about the same subject. For example, if two authors write about trains, each might create a different picture. One might present trains as destructive machines. The other might show them as a means of bringing people together.

When reading a story, the glasses created by an author often allow you to see

- the world through a character's eyes

- what someone else's life is like

- your past experiences in a new way

- familiar things as though they were brand new

QUESTIONS FOR READING FICTION

As you read the next three stories, keep the following questions in mind.

1. What does the author allow you to see and understand about the main character's life and personality?

2. How does the author describe important issues such as growing up, making friends, and being truthful?

3. What parts of your own life does the author make you think about?

4. What new ideas do you have after reading the story?

5. How would you describe the view of life presented in the story—depressing? hopeful? humorous? something else?

CHARLES

by Shirley Jackson

As you read: Find out who Charles really is.

The day my son Laurie started kindergarten he renounced corduroy overalls with bibs and began wearing blue jeans with a belt; I watched him go off the first morning with the older girl next door, seeing clearly that an era of my life was ended, my sweet-voiced nursery-school tot replaced by a long-trousered, swaggering character who forgot to stop at the corner and wave goodbye to me.

He came home the same way, the front door slamming open, his cap on the floor, and the voice suddenly become raucous shouting, "Isn't anybody *here?*"

At lunch he spoke insolently to his father, spilled his baby sister's milk, and remarked that his teacher said we were not to take the name of the Lord in vain.

"How *was* school today?" I asked, elaborately casual.

"All right," he said.

"Did you learn anything?" his father asked.

Laurie regarded his father coldly. "I didn't learn nothing," he said.

"Anything," I said. "Didn't learn anything."

"The teacher spanked a boy, though," Laurie said, addressing his bread and butter. "For being fresh," he added, with his mouth full.

"What did he do?" I asked. "Who was it?"

Laurie thought. "It was Charles," he said. "He

was fresh. The teacher spanked him and made him stand in a corner. He was awfully fresh."

"What did he do?" I asked again, but Laurie slid off his chair, took a cookie, and left, while his father was still saying, "See here, young man."

The next day Laurie remarked at lunch, as soon as he sat down, "Well, Charles was bad again today." He grinned enormously and said, "Today Charles hit the teacher."

"Good heavens," I said, mindful of the Lord's name, "I suppose he got spanked again?"

"He sure did," Laurie said. "Look up," he said to his father.

"What?" his father said, looking up.

"Look down," Laurie said. "Look at my thumb. Gee, you're dumb." He began to laugh insanely.

"Why did Charles hit the teacher?" I asked quickly.

"Because she tried to make him color with red crayons," Laurie said. "Charles wanted to color with green crayons so he hit the teacher and she spanked him and said nobody play with Charles but everybody did."

The third day—it was Wednesday of the first week—Charles bounced a seesaw onto the head of a little girl and made her bleed, and the teacher made him stay inside all during recess. Thursday Charles had to stand in a corner during

Making Sense • FICTION

story time because he kept pounding his feet on the floor. Friday Charles was deprived of blackboard privileges because he threw chalk.

On Saturday I remarked to my husband, "Do you think kindergarten is too unsettling for Laurie? All this toughness, and bad grammar, and this Charles boy sounds like such a bad influence."

"It'll be all right," my husband said reassuringly. "Bound to be people like Charles in the world. Might as well meet them now as later."

On Monday Laurie came home late, full of news. "Charles," he shouted as he came up the hill; I was waiting anxiously on the front steps. "Charles," Laurie yelled all the way up the hill, "Charles was bad again."

"Come right in," I said, as soon as he came close enough. "Lunch is waiting."

"You know what Charles did?" he demanded, following me through the door. "Charles yelled so in school they sent a boy in from first grade to tell the teacher she had to make Charles keep quiet, and so Charles had to stay after school. And so all the children stayed to watch him."

"What did he do?" I asked.

"He just sat there," Laurie said, climbing into his chair at the table. "Hi, Pop, y'old dust mop."

"Charles had to stay after school today," I told my husband. "Everyone stayed with him."

"What does this Charles look like?" my husband asked Laurie. "What's his other name?"

"He's bigger than me," Laurie said. "And he doesn't have any rubbers and he doesn't ever wear a jacket."

Monday night was the first Parent-Teachers meeting, and only the fact that the baby had a cold kept me from going; I wanted passionately to meet Charles's mother. On Tuesday Laurie remarked suddenly, "Our teacher had a friend come to see her in school today."

"Charles's mother?" my husband and I asked simultaneously.

"Naaah," Laurie said scornfully. "It was a man who came and made us do exercises, we had to touch our toes. Look." He climbed down from his chair and squatted down and touched his toes. "Like this," he said. He got solemnly back into his chair and said, picking up his fork, "Charles didn't even *do* exercises."

"That's fine," I said heartily. "Didn't Charles want to do exercises?"

"Naaah," Laurie said, "Charles was so fresh to the teacher's friend he wasn't *let* do exercises."

"Fresh again?" I said.

"He kicked the teacher's friend," Laurie said. "The teacher's friend told Charles to touch his toes like I just did and Charles kicked him."

"What are they going to do about Charles, do you suppose?" Laurie's father asked him.

Laurie shrugged elaborately. "Throw him out of school, I guess," he said.

Wednesday and Thursday were routine; Charles yelled during story hour and hit a boy in the stomach and made him cry. On Friday Charles stayed after school again and so did all the other children.

With the third week of kindergarten Charles was an institution in our family; the baby was being a Charles when she cried all afternoon; Laurie did a Charles when he filled his wagon full of mud and pulled it through the kitchen; even my husband, when he caught his elbow in the telephone cord and pulled telephone, ashtray, and a bowl of flowers off the table, said, after the first minute, "Looks like Charles."

During the third and fourth weeks it looked like a reformation in Charles; Laurie reported grimly at lunch on Thursday of the third week, "Charles was so good today the teacher gave him an apple."

"What?" I said, and my husband added warily, "You mean Charles?"

"Charles," Laurie said. "He gave the crayons

around and he picked up the books afterward and the teacher said he was her helper."

"What happened?" I asked incredulously.

"He was her helper, that's all," Laurie said, and shrugged.

"Can this be true, about Charles?" I asked my husband that night. "Can something like this happen?"

"Wait and see," my husband said cynically. "When you've got a Charles to deal with, this may mean he's only plotting."

He seemed to be wrong. For over a week Charles was the teacher's helper; each day he handed things out and he picked things up; no one had to stay after school.

"The P.T.A. meeting's next week again," I told my husband one evening. "I'm going to find Charles's mother there."

"Ask her what happened to Charles," my husband said. "I'd like to know."

"I'd like to know myself," I said.

On Friday of that week things were back to normal. "You know what Charles did today?" Laurie demanded at the lunch table, in a voice slightly awed. "He told a little girl to say a word and she said it and the teacher washed her mouth out with soap and Charles laughed."

"What word?" his father asked unwisely, and Laurie said, "I'll have to whisper it to you, it's so bad." He got down off his chair and went around to his father. His father bent his head down and Laurie whispered joyfully. His father's eyes widened.

"Did Charles tell the little girl to say *that*?" he asked respectfully.

"She said it *twice*," Laurie said. "Charles told her to say it *twice*."

"What happened to Charles?" my husband asked.

"Nothing," Laurie said. "He was passing out the crayons."

Monday morning Charles abandoned the little girl and said the evil word himself three or four times, getting his mouth washed out with soap each time. He also threw chalk.

My husband came to the door with me that evening as I set out for the P.T.A. meeting. "Invite her over for a cup of tea after the meeting," he said. "I want to get a look at her."

"If only she's there," I said prayerfully.

"She'll be there," my husband said. "I don't see how they could hold a P.T.A. meeting without Charles's mother."

At the meeting I sat restlessly, scanning each comfortable matronly face, trying to determine which one hid the secret of Charles. None of them looked to me haggard enough. No one stood up in the meeting and apologized for the way her son had been acting. No one mentioned Charles.

After the meeting I identified and sought out Laurie's kindergarten teacher. She had a plate with a cup of tea and a piece of chocolate cake; I had a plate with a cup of tea and a piece of marshmallow cake. We maneuvered up to one another cautiously, and smiled.

"I've been so anxious to meet you," I said. "I'm Laurie's mother."

"We're all so interested in Laurie," she said.

"Well, he certainly likes kindergarten," I said. "He talks about it all the time."

"We had a little trouble adjusting, the first week or so," she said primly, "but now he's a fine little helper. With occasional lapses, of course."

"Laurie usually adjusts very quickly," I said. "I suppose this time it's Charles's influence."

"Charles?"

"Yes," I said, laughing, "you must have your hands full in that kindergarten, with Charles."

"Charles?" she said. "We don't have any Charles in the kindergarten."

Using Context Clues

Directions: Each of the passages below contains a word in **bold** print. As you read each excerpt, look for clues that might help you decide on the meaning of the bold-faced word. Choose the letter of the best response.

Excerpt 1

"The day my son Laurie started kindergarten he **renounced** corduroy overalls with bibs and began wearing blue jeans with a belt; I watched him go off the first morning with the older girl next door, seeing clearly that an era of my life was ended, my sweet-voiced nursery-school tot replaced by a long-trousered, swaggering character who forgot to stop at the corner and wave goodbye to me."

1. When Charles **renounces** overalls, he

      Ⓐ wears them   Ⓒ ruins them

      Ⓑ rejects them   Ⓓ buys them

Excerpt 2

"During the third and fourth weeks it looked like a **reformation** in Charles; Laurie reported grimly at lunch on Thursday of the third week, "Charles was so good today the teacher gave him an apple.""

2. When Charles undergoes a **reformation,** he

      Ⓐ improves his behavior   Ⓒ returns to normal

      Ⓑ changes for the worse   Ⓓ makes a choice without thinking

Excerpt 3

"Can this be true, about Charles?" I asked my husband that night. "Can something like this happen?" "Wait and see," my husband said **cynically.** "When you've got a Charles to deal with, this may mean he's only plotting.""

3. When Charles' father answers **cynically,** he is showing

      Ⓐ disappointment   Ⓒ joy

      Ⓑ doubt   Ⓓ anger

Getting the Main Idea

Directions: Each of the passages below summarizes a part of the story. Read the passage; then choose the sentence that best states the main idea of the passage.

1. Laurie's mother asks her husband if he thinks that Charles is a bad influence on Laurie. Her husband reassures her that Laurie is bound to meet many other people like Charles during his life.

   Ⓐ Laurie's parents think their son is a bad boy who learns to misbehave at school.

   Ⓑ Laurie's parents believe their son should be taken out of kindergarten.

   Ⓒ Laurie's parents feel Laurie has a lot to gain from his school experiences.

   Ⓓ Laurie's parents see their son as a good boy who has made bad friends.

2. By the third week of kindergarten, the name Charles takes on new meanings in Laurie's household. Whenever the baby cries for long periods, she becomes a Charles. When Laurie is careless, he is a Charles. When Laurie's father accidentally knocks over a bowl of flowers, he points to the mess and says, "It looks like Charles."

   Ⓐ The family believes that Charles is responsible for their mistakes.

   Ⓑ The family jokes that its members sometimes act like Charles.

   Ⓒ The family confuses the baby's crying with Charles's wails.

   Ⓓ The family grows tired of Charles's bad influence on Laurie, even at home.

3. At the P.T.A. meeting, Laurie's mother finds Laurie's kindergarten teacher and introduces herself. The teacher makes a favorable remark about Laurie; she then says he had a little trouble earlier in the school year. Laurie's mother mentions how quickly Laurie adjusts and suggests that Charles's influence is to blame. The teacher says that there is no student by the name of Charles in her kindergarten class.

   Ⓐ The teacher says that Laurie's behavior has improved and she doesn't know Charles.

   Ⓑ The teacher agrees that Laurie has adjusted well to kindergarten.

   Ⓒ The teacher denies she knows Charles to protect Laurie's mother.

   Ⓓ The teacher blames Laurie's misbehavior on Charles.

Who Is Charles?

The author never says who Charles is. Instead she leaves it up to the reader to decide.

Directions: Decide whether Charles is really Laurie or a person Laurie made up. Then give at least two details or statements from the story to support your opinion. Use what you know about children and getting in trouble to complete the last box.

Charles is	Ⓐ really Laurie	Ⓑ a person Laurie made up

1. List two details from the story that prove who Charles is.

2. List two things from your own experience that prove who Charles is.

PRISCILLA AND THE WIMPS

Prereading: Making Predictions

One of the characters in "Priscilla and the Wimps" is a bully. Use what you know about bullies to predict what might happen in this story.

Directions: Use the left-hand column to record your predictions before reading. After you finish the story, use the right-hand column to record what actually happened in the story.

Before Reading	After Reading
1. How do you think the bully will treat other kids?	1. How does the bully treat other kids in the story?
2. Lists some ways that other kids will react to the bully.	2. How do other kids react to the bully in the story?
3. Predict who will have the upper hand at the end of the story—the bully or the victims.	3. Who has the upper hand at the end of the story?

Summing It Up

Do you enjoy reading a story more when your predictions are fulfilled or when something you didn't expect happens? Explain.

_____

_____

PRISCILLA AND THE WIMPS

by Richard Peck

As you read: Find out whether your predictions about bullies are accurate.

Listen, there was a time when you couldn't even go to the *rest room* around this school without a pass. And I'm not talking about those little pink tickets made out by some teacher. I'm talking about a pass that could cost anywhere up to a buck, sold by Monk Klutter.

Not that Mighty Monk ever touched money, not in public. The gang he ran, which ran the school for him, was his collection agency. They were Klutter's Kobras, a name spelled out in nailheads on six well-known black plastic windbreakers.

Monk's threads were more…subtle. A pile-lined suede battle jacket with lizard-skin flaps over tailored Levis and a pair of ostrich-skin boots, brassed-toed and suitable for kicking people around. One of his Kobras did nothing all day but walk a half step behind Monk, carrying a fitted bag with Monk's gym shoes, a roll of rest-room passes, a cashbox, and a switchblade that Monk gave himself manicures with at lunch over at the Kobras' table.

Speaking of lunch, there were a few cases of advanced malnutrition among the newer kids. The ones who were a little slow in handing over a cut of their lunch money and were therefore barred from the cafeteria. Monk ran a tight ship.

I admit it. I'm five foot five, and when the Kobras slithered by, with or without Monk, I shrank. And I admit this, too: I paid up on a regular basis. And I might add: so would you.

This school was old Monk's Garden of Eden. Unfortunately for him, there was a serpent in it. The reason Monk didn't recognize trouble when it was staring him in the face is that the serpent in the Kobra's Eden was a girl.

Practically every guy in school could show you his scars. Fang marks from Kobras, you might say. And they were all highly visible in the shower room: lumps, lacerations, blue bruises, you name it. But girls usually got off with a warning.

Except there was this one girl named Priscilla Roseberry. Picture a girl named Priscilla Roseberry, and you'll be light years off. Priscilla was, hands down, the largest student in our particular institution of learning. I'm not talking fat, I'm talking big. Even beautiful, in a bionic way. Priscilla wasn't inclined toward organized crime. Otherwise, she could have put together a gang that would turn Klutter's Kobras into garter snakes.

Priscilla was basically a loner except she had one friend. A little guy named Melvin Detweiler. You talk about The Odd Couple. Melvin's one of the smallest guys above midget status ever seen. A really nice guy, but, you know—little. They even had lockers next to each other, in the same bank as mine. I don't know what they had going. I'm not saying this was a romance. After all, people deserve their privacy.

Priscilla was sort of above everything, if you'll pardon a pun. And very calm, as only the very big can be. If there was anybody who didn't notice Klutter's Kobras, it was Priscilla.

Until one winter day after school when we were all grabbing our coats out of our lockers. And hurrying, since Klutter's Kobras made sweeps of the halls for after-school shakedowns.

Anyway, up to Melvin's locker swaggers one of the Kobras. Never mind his name. Gang members don't need names. They've got group identity. He reaches down and grabs little Melvin by the neck and slams his head against his locker door. The sound of skull against steel rippled all the way down the locker row, speeding the crowds on their way.

"Okay, let's see your pass," snarls the Kobra.

"A pass for what this time?" Melvin asks, probably still dazed.

"Let's call it a pass for very short people," says the Kobra, "a dwarf tax." He wheezes a little Kobra chuckle at his own wittiness. And already he's reaching for Melvin's wallet with the hand that isn't circling Melvin's windpipe. All this time, of course, Melvin and the Kobra are standing in Priscilla's big shadow.

She's taking her time shoving her books into her locker and pulling on a very large-size coat. Then, quicker than the eye, she brings the side of her enormous hand down in a chop that breaks the Kobra's hold on Melvin's throat. You could hear a pin drop in that hallway. Nobody'd ever laid a finger on a Kobra, let alone a hand the size of Priscilla's.

Then Priscilla, who hardly ever says anything to anybody except to Melvin, says to the Kobra, "Who's your leader, wimp?"

This practically blows the Kobra away. First

he's chopped by a girl, and now she's acting like she doesn't know Monk Klutter, the Head Honcho of the World. He's so amazed, he tells her. "Monk Klutter."

"Never heard of him," Priscilla mentions. "Send him to see me." The Kobra just backs away from her like the whole situation is too big for him, which it is.

Pretty soon Monk himself slides up. He jerks his head once, and his Kobras slither off down the hall. He's going to handle this interesting case personally. "Who is it around here doesn't know Monk Klutter?"

He's standing inches from Priscilla, but since he'd have to look up at her, he doesn't. "Never heard of him," says Priscilla.

Monk's not happy with this answer, but by now he's spotted Melvin, who's grown smaller in spite of himself. Monk breaks his own rule by reaching for Melvin with his own hands. "Kid," he says, "you're going to have to educate your girlfriend."

His hands never quite make it to Melvin. In a move of pure poetry Priscilla has Monk in a hammerlock. His neck's popping like gunfire, and his head's bowed under the immense weight of her forearm. His suede jacket's peeling back, showing pile.

Priscilla's behind him in another easy motion. And with a single mighty thrust forward, frogmarches Monk into her own locker. It's incredible. His ostrich-skin boots click once in the air. And suddenly he's gone, neatly wedged into the locker, a perfect fit. Priscilla bangs the door shut, twirls the lock, and strolls out of school. Melvin goes with her, of course, trotting along below her shoulder. The last stragglers leave quietly.

Well, this is where fate, an even bigger force than Priscilla, steps in. It snows all that night, a blizzard. The whole town ices up. And school closes for a week.

Slang and Informal Language

The narrator of "Priscilla and the Wimps" uses many colorful expressions. Some are slang terms and others are simply informal language.

Directions: Rewrite the following sentences by replacing the bold-faced word or phrase with an everyday expression that has the same meaning. The first one is done for you.

1. This school was old Monk's **Garden of Eden.**

    This school was Monk's territory, his personal paradise.

2. Monk's **threads** were more…subtle.

    _____

3. Monk ran a **tight ship.**

    _____

4. Klutter's Kobras made sweeps of the halls for after-school **shakedowns.**

    _____

5. Priscilla wasn't inclined toward **organized crime.**

    _____

6. He jerks his head once, and his Kobras **slither off** down the hall.

    _____

7. In a move of **pure poetry** Priscilla has Monk in a hammerlock.

    _____

8. Priscilla's behind him in another easy motion. And with a single mighty thrust forward, **frog-marches** Monk into her own locker.

    _____

Making Inferences

An *inference* is an "educated guess" or logical conclusion based on clues in a piece of writing.

Directions: As you read the following passages from "Priscilla and the Wimps," look carefully at the author's choice of words and details. Use these clues to infer the answers to the questions that follow.

Passage 1

I admit it. I'm five foot five, and when the Kobras slithered by, with or without Monk, I shrank. And I admit this, too: I paid up on a regular basis. And I might add: so would you.

1. What is the narrator's relationship to the Kobras?

    Ⓐ He feels equal to the Kobras.
    Ⓒ He wants to become a Kobra.
    Ⓑ He feels powerless before the Kobras.
    Ⓓ He ignores the Kobras.

2. Underline the words in Passage 1 on which you based your choice.

Passage 2

Then Priscilla, who hardly ever says anything to anybody except to Melvin, says to the Kobra, "Who's your leader, wimp?"

3. What is Priscilla's relationship to the Kobra?

    Ⓐ She thinks the Kobra is a coward.
    Ⓒ She likes the Kobra.
    Ⓑ She thinks the Kobra is a threat.
    Ⓓ She ignores the Kobra.

4. Underline the words in Passage 2 on which you based your choice.

Passage 3

Monk breaks his own rule by reaching for Melvin with his own hands. "Kid," he says, "you're going to have to educate your girlfriend."

5. How does Monk view Priscilla?

    Ⓐ He fears her.
    Ⓒ He thinks he can overpower her.
    Ⓑ He likes her because she is tall.
    Ⓓ He wants her in his gang.

6. Underline the words in Passage 3 on which you based your choice.

Passage 4

In a move of pure poetry Priscilla has Monk in a hammerlock. His neck's popping like gunfire, and his head's bowed under the immense weight of her forearm.

7. How does the narrator view Priscilla?

    Ⓐ He is in love with her.   Ⓒ He fears her.

    Ⓑ He dislikes her because she is tall.   Ⓓ He respects and admires her.

8. Underline the words in Passage 4 on which you based your choice.

Passage 5

Well, this is where fate, an even bigger force than Priscilla, steps in. It snows all that night, a blizzard. The whole town ices up. And school closes for a week.

9. What does the narrator imply happens to Monk?

    Ⓐ Monk runs from Priscilla.   Ⓒ Monk is trapped for a week.

    Ⓑ The Kobras rescue Monk.   Ⓓ Monk is no longer a bully.

10. Underline the words in Passage 5 on which you based your choice.

Your Turn

Here is space for your personal reaction to "Priscilla and the Wimps."

THE NO-GUITAR BLUES

by Gary Soto

As you read: Watch for ways Fausto learns from his experience.

The moment Fausto saw the group Los Lobos on "American Bandstand," he knew exactly what he wanted to do with his life—play guitar. His eyes grew large with excitement as Los Lobos ground out a song while teenagers bounced off each other on the crowded dance floor.

He had watched "American Bandstand" for years and had heard Ray Camacho and the Teardrops at Romain Playground, but it had never occurred to him that he too might become a musician. That afternoon Fausto knew his mission in life: to play guitar in his own band; to sweat out his songs and prance around the stage; to make money and dress weird.

Fausto turned off the television set and walked outside, wondering how he could get enough money to buy a guitar. He couldn't ask his parents because they would just say, "Money doesn't grow on trees" or "What do you think we are, bankers?" And besides, they hated rock music. They were into the *conjunto* music of Lydia Mendoza, Flaco Jimenez, and Little Joe and La Familia. And, as Fausto recalled, the last album they bought was *The Chipmunks Sing Christmas Favorites.*

But what the heck, he'd give it a try. He returned inside and watched his mother make tortillas. He leaned against the kitchen counter, trying to work up the nerve to ask her for a guitar. Finally, he couldn't hold back any longer.

"Mom," he said, "I want a guitar for Christmas."

She looked up from rolling tortillas. "Honey, a guitar costs a lot of money."

"How 'bout for my birthday next year," he tried again.

"I can't promise," she said, turning back to her tortillas, "but we'll see."

Fausto walked back outside with a buttered tortilla. He knew his mother was right. His father was a warehouseman at Berven Rugs, where he made good money but not enough to buy everything his children wanted. Fausto decided to mow lawns to earn money, and was pushing the mower down the street before he realized it was winter and no one would hire him. He returned the mower and picked up a rake. He hopped onto his sister's bike (his had two flat tires) and rode north to the nicer section of Fresno in search of work. He went door-to-door, but after three hours he managed to get only one job, and not to rake leaves. He was asked to hurry down to the store to buy a loaf of bread, for which he received a grimy, dirt-caked quarter.

He also got an orange, which he ate sitting at the curb. While he was eating, a dog walked up and sniffed his leg. Fausto pushed him away and threw an orange peel skyward. The dog caught it and ate it in one gulp. The dog looked at Fausto and wagged his tail for more. Fausto tossed him a slice of orange, and the dog snapped it up and licked his lips.

"How come you like oranges, dog?"

The dog blinked a pair of sad eyes and whined.

"What's the matter? Cat got your tongue?" Fausto laughed at his joke and offered the dog another slice.

At that moment a dim light came on inside Fausto's head. He saw that it was sort of a fancy dog, a terrier or something, with dog tags and a shiny collar. And it looked well fed and healthy. In his neighborhood, the dogs were never licensed, and if they got sick they were placed near the water heater until they got well.

This dog looked like he belonged to rich people. Fausto cleaned his juice-sticky hands on his pants and got to his feet. The light in his head grew brighter. It just might work. He called the dog, patted its muscular back, and bent down to check the license.

"Great," he said. "There's an address."

The dog's name was Roger, which struck Fausto as weird because he had never heard of a dog with a human name. Dogs should have names like Bomber, Freckles, Queenie, Killer, and Zero.

Fausto planned to take the dog home and collect a reward. He would say he had found Roger near the freeway. That would scare the daylights out of the owners, who would be so happy that they would probably give him a reward. He felt bad about lying, but the dog *was* loose. And it might even really be lost, because the address was six blocks away.

Fausto stashed the rake and his sister's bike behind a bush, and, tossing an orange peel every time Roger became distracted, walked the dog to his house. He hesitated on the porch until Roger began to scratch the door with a muddy paw. Fausto had come this far, so he figured he might as well go through with it. He knocked softly.

When no one answered, he rang the doorbell. A man in a silky bathrobe and slippers opened the door and seemed confused by the sight of his dog and the boy.

"Sir," Fausto said, gripping Roger by the collar. "I found your dog by the freeway. His dog license says he lives here." Fausto looked down at the dog, then up to the man. "He does, doesn't he?"

The man stared at Fausto a long time before saying in a pleasant voice, "That's right." He pulled his robe tighter around him because of the cold and asked Fausto to come in. "So he was by the freeway?"

"Uh-huh."

"You bad, snoopy dog," said the man, wagging his finger. "You probably knocked over some trash cans, too, didn't you?"

Fausto didn't say anything. He looked around, amazed by this house with its shiny furniture and a television as large as the front window at home. Warm bread smells filled the air and music full of soft tinkling floated in from another room.

"Helen," the man called to the kitchen. "We have a visitor." His wife came into the living room wiping her hands on a dish towel and smiling. "And who have we here?" she asked in one of the softest voices Fausto had ever heard.

"This young man said he found Roger near the freeway."

Fausto repeated his story to her while staring at a perpetual clock with a bell-shaped glass, the kind his aunt got when she celebrated her twenty-fifth anniversary. The lady frowned and said, wagging a finger at Roger, "Oh, you're a bad boy."

"It was very nice of you to bring Roger home," the man said. "Where do you live?"

"By that vacant lot on Olive," he said. "You know, by Brownie's Flower Place."

The wife looked at her husband, then Fausto. Her eyes twinkled triangles of light as she said,

"Well, young man, you're probably hungry. How about a turnover?"

"What do I have to turn over?" Fausto asked, thinking she was talking about yard work or something like turning over trays of dried raisins.

"No, no, dear, it's a pastry." She took him by the elbow and guided him to a kitchen that sparkled with copper pans and bright yellow wallpaper. She guided him to the kitchen table and gave him a tall glass of milk and something that looked like an *empanada*. Steamy waves of heat escaped when he tore it in two. He ate with both eyes on the man and woman who stood arm in arm smiling at him. They were strange, he thought. But nice.

"That was good," he said after he finished the turnover. "Did you make it, ma'am?"

"Yes, I did. Would you like another?"

"No, thank you. I have to go home now."

As Fausto walked to the door, the man opened his wallet and took out a bill. "This is for you," he said. "Roger is very special to us, almost like a son."

Fausto looked at the bill and knew he was in trouble. Not with these nice folks or with his parents but with himself. How could he have been so deceitful? The dog wasn't lost. It was just having a fun Saturday walking around.

"I can't take that."

"You have to. You deserve it, believe me," the man said.

"No, I don't."

"Now don't be silly," said the lady. She took the bill from her husband and stuffed it into Fausto's shirt pocket. "You're a lovely child. Your parents are lucky to have you. Be good. And come see us again, please."

Fausto went out, and the lady closed the door. Fausto clutched the bill through his shirt pocket. He felt like ringing the doorbell and begging them to please take the money back, but he knew they would refuse. He hurried away, and at the end of the block, pulled the bill from his shirt pocket: it was a crisp twenty-dollar bill.

"Oh, man, I shouldn't have lied," he said under his breath as he started up the street like a zombie. He wanted to run to church for Saturday confession, but it was past four-thirty, when confession stopped.

He returned to the bush where he had hidden the rake and his sister's bike and rode home slowly, not daring to touch the money in his pocket. At home, in the privacy of his room, he examined the twenty-dollar bill. He had never had so much money. It was probably enough to buy a second-hand guitar. But he felt bad, like the time he stole a dollar from the secret fold inside his older brother's wallet.

Fausto went outside and sat on the fence. "Yeah," he said. "I can probably get a guitar for twenty. Maybe at a yard sale—things are cheaper."

His mother called him to dinner.

The next day he dressed for church without anyone telling him. He was going to go to eight o'clock mass.

"I'm going to church, Mom," he said. His mother was in the kitchen cooking *papas* and *chorizo con huevos*. A pile of tortillas lay warm under a dishtowel.

"Oh, I'm so proud of you, my son." She beamed, turning over the crackling *papas*.

His older brother, Lawrence, who was at the table reading the funnies, mimicked, "Oh, I'm so proud of you, my son," under his breath.

At Saint Theresa's he sat near the front. When Father Jerry began by saying that we are all sinners, Fausto thought he looked straight at him. Could he know? Fausto fidgeted with guilt. No, he thought. I only did it yesterday.

Fausto knelt, prayed, and sang. But he couldn't forget the man and the lady, whose names he didn't even know, and the *empanada* they had given him. It had a strange name but tasted really good. He wondered how they got rich. And how that dome clock worked. He had asked his mother once how his aunt's clock worked. She said it just worked, the way the refrigerator works. It just did.

Fausto caught his mind wandering and tried to concentrate on his sins. He said a Hail Mary and sang, and when the wicker basket came his way, he stuck a hand reluctantly in his pocket and pulled out the twenty-dollar bill. He ironed it between his palms, and dropped it into the basket. The grownups stared. Here was a kid dropping twenty dollars in the basket while they gave just three or four dollars.

There would be a second collection for Saint Vincent de Paul, the lector announced. The wicker baskets again floated in the pews, and this time the adults around him, given a second chance to show their charity, dug deep into their wallets and purses and dropped in fives and tens. This time Fausto tossed in the grimy quarter.

Fausto felt better after church. He went home and played football in the front yard with his brother and some neighbor kids. He felt cleared of wrongdoing and was so happy that he played one of his best games of football ever. On one play, he tore his good pants, which he knew he shouldn't have been wearing. For a second, while he examined the hole, he wished he hadn't given the twenty dollars away.

Man, I coulda bought me some Levi's, he thought. He pictured his twenty dollars being spent to buy church candles. He pictured a priest buying an armful of flowers with *his* money.

Fausto had to forget about getting a guitar. He spent the next day playing soccer in his good pants, which were now his old pants. But that night during dinner, his mother said she remembered seeing an old bass guitarron the last time she cleaned out her father's garage.

"It's a little dusty," his mom said, serving his favorite enchiladas. "But I think it works. Grandpa says it works."

Fausto's ears perked up. That was the same kind the guy in Los Lobos played. Instead of asking for the guitar, he waited for his mother to offer it to him. And she did, while gathering the dishes from the table.

"No, Mom, I'll do it," he said, hugging her. "I'll do the dishes forever if you want."

It was the happiest day of his life. No, it was the second-happiest day of his life. The happiest was when his grandfather Lupe placed the guitarron, which was nearly as huge as a washtub, in his arms. Fausto ran a thumb down the strings, which vibrated in his throat and chest. It sounded beautiful, deep and eerie. A pumpkin smile widened on his face.

"Okay, *hijo,* now you put your fingers like this," said his grandfather, smelling of tobacco and aftershave. He took Fausto's fingers and placed them on the strings. Fausto strummed a chord on the guitarron, and the bass resounded in their chests.

The guitarron was more complicated than Fausto imagined. But he was confident that after a few more lessons he could start a band that would someday play on "American Bandstand" for the dancing crowds.

Cause and Effect

In "The No-Guitar Blues," Fausto lies about helping a dog. The author of the story suggests the reason why Fausto lies, or the *cause* of his action. The author also demonstrates the impact of Fausto's lie, or its *effects*.

Directions: In the spaces provided on the right below, write two effects of Fausto's lie.

1.

Effects

Cause

Fausto wants a guitar and cannot afford to buy one.

Fausto Lies

2. What do you think the effects of the lie reveal about the author's view of honesty? _____

_____

_____

_____

3. Do you think Fausto had good reasons to lie? Explain your response. _____

_____

_____

_____

Internal Conflicts

In "The No-Guitar Blues" the character Fausto experiences several internal conflicts. *Internal conflicts* occur when characters clash with forces inside themselves, such as fear or conscience.

Directions: Read the two internal conflicts Fausto faces. Then answer the questions that follow about how the conflicts are ended or *resolved*.

1. **Conflict:** Fausto wants a guitar but cannot afford to buy one.

How is this conflict resolved?

Ⓐ Fausto goes to work and eventually buys a guitar.

Ⓑ Fausto "rescues" a dog and is paid a $20.00 reward.

Ⓒ Fausto steals a guitar from a friend.

Ⓓ Fausto's grandfather shows him how to play his old guitarron.

How does this resolution affect Fausto? _____

_____

_____

2. **Conflict:** Fausto feels guilty when a wealthy couple pays him for a job he didn't do.

How does Fausto resolve this conflict?

Ⓐ He asks the couple for forgiveness.

Ⓑ He goes to confession and asks for forgiveness.

Ⓒ He tells his parents about his wrongdoing and returns the money.

Ⓓ He gives the money to his church.

How does this resolution affect Fausto? _____

_____

_____

_____

Details That Reveal Character

Directions: These passages describe Fausto's feelings or attitude toward the events in the story. Choose the sentence that best captures Fausto's feelings.

1. "The moment Fausto saw the group Los Lobos on 'American Bandstand,' he knew exactly what he wanted to do with his life—play guitar. His eyes grew large with excitement as Los Lobos ground out a song while teenagers bounced off each other…."

   Ⓐ Fausto dislikes "American Bandstand."

   Ⓑ Fausto wants to quit school and join a band.

   Ⓒ Fausto has found what he wants to do with his life.

   Ⓓ Fausto likes to watch television.

2. "Fausto didn't say anything. He looked around, amazed by this house with its shiny furniture and a television as large as the front window at home."

   Ⓐ Fausto feels depressed because he is poor compared to the dog's owners.

   Ⓑ Fausto wants to live with the couple who own the dog.

   Ⓒ Fausto is impressed by the rich surroundings.

   Ⓓ Fausto is tempted to steal something from the wealthy couple's house.

3. "Fausto looked at the bill and knew he was in trouble. Not with these nice folks or with his parents but with himself. How could he have been so deceitful? The dog wasn't lost. It was just having a fun Saturday walking around."

   Ⓐ Fausto feels bad about taking the dog's fun away from him.

   Ⓑ Fausto is afraid that someone will discover his lie.

   Ⓒ Fausto is trying to decide how he can apologize to the dog's owners.

   Ⓓ Fausto feels guilty about lying to the nice couple.

4. "Fausto felt better after church. He went home and played football in the front yard with his brother and some neighbor kids. He felt cleared of wrongdoing and was so happy that he played one of his best games of football ever."

   Ⓐ Fausto feels that he will never be forgiven.

   Ⓑ Fausto feels that he is forgiven for lying.

   Ⓒ Fausto uses the football game to forget about the lie.

   Ⓓ Fausto strongly wants to get over the lie.

Reading Myths and Folktales

Myths both entertain and instruct. They contain events and characters that appeal to our imaginations—animals that talk, people that fly, and trees that laugh. Myths also provide answers to basic human questions. They help explain why human suffering exists, why there are different seasons, and how thunder is created.

Folktales are similar to myths in many ways. Both myths and folktales were told as stories long before they were written down. Both contain imaginary characters. However, folktales are often about animals that talk and act like people. Myths are often about gods and heroes. And myths and folktales explain different things. Myths explore questions about nature and human experience. Folktales teach important lessons or morals. They might show how a poor person can use his wits to succeed or the importance of working together.

TIPS FOR READING MYTHS AND FOLKTALES

As you read, pay attention to these three features.

1) **Characters**
   If the characters are gods and heroes, you're probably reading a myth. If they're ordinary people or talking animals, you're more likely to be reading a folktale.

2) **Events**
   The events in myths often describe the actions of the gods and the way gods and humans interact. Events in folktales often describe the relationships between animals or a fanciful situation.

3) **Lessons**
   Myths often explain nature or answer important human questions, such as how evil came into the world. Folktales, on the other hand, teach morals or lessons.

PANDORA'S BOX

A tale from ancient Greece
as retold by Cynthia M. Martin

As you read: Decide what you would have done in Pandora's place.

Zeus, the king of the gods, was angry. In fact, he was furious, and when Zeus was enraged, nobody was happy. He paced back and forth in his home on Mount Olympus, frowning and muttering to himself.

"That Prometheus," he growled. "He stole *my* fire and gave it to those miserable, puny humans! Now they think they're as good as the gods! They must be punished!"

Hermes sat in a corner, watching Zeus as the ruler ranted and raved. Hermes was the messenger for the gods, who spent his time flying between heaven and earth, carrying Zeus's orders to the universe. He always gave Zeus excellent advice. "You can't blame Prometheus," he said quietly. "You know how much he adores the humans."

"Yes, but I don't understand why," said Zeus. "They're pathetically slow and stupid, and they're always whining and begging us for help."

"But Prometheus loves them," replied Hermes. "He feels sorry for them. They were hungry from living on nothing but roots and berries. They had no light at night except for the moon. They had no way to warm their houses. They couldn't defend themselves from wild animals. Now they are warm. They can use fire to cook meat. They can keep the wild animals from attacking them.

I'm sure Prometheus thought it was worth the risk."

"I doubt he still believes that," Zeus said sarcastically.

"No, I'm sure that he's sorry now," Hermes replied. "After all, you chained him to that rock. He has to stand there, buffeted by the wind, soaked by the rain, and broiled by the sun. Not only that, but you send an eagle to rip out his liver every night. *Then* it grows back so the eagle can come and rip it out again." He shuddered. "That's a savage punishment."

"Are you telling me what I can and can't do?" Zeus roared. He scowled at Hermes, his eyes glowing with rage. "Are you telling me that… that I should feel sorry for that human-loving traitor?"

"Oh, no, no," Hermes said quickly, laughing nervously. "No one can deny that you had the right to punish Prometheus, oh king of all the gods. But I can't see how you can punish all the humans at once."

"Hmmm," Zeus said, "you're right, oh winged one." He thought about it for a minute. "Wait!" He grinned. "I know just what to do. I can trap Prometheus's brother, Epimetheus. He isn't very bright. I'll send him a gift, a *very* special gift. He won't suspect a thing. I can punish him, and I can

use *him* to punish the humans. They had no business taking the fire Prometheus gave them."

Zeus chuckled nastily. He rubbed his hands with glee at the thought of revenging himself on all the humans. "Leave me, Hermes. Call all the gods and goddesses together. I'll need their help."

Then Zeus went to work. He created a young woman and named her Pandora. The other gods arrived just as he finished his creation.

"You wished to see us, Mighty Thunderer?" Athena asked. She was Zeus's daughter, the goddess of wisdom.

"What is it now?" Aphrodite, the goddess of love, sighed. "I was just getting ready to fly down to Earth and make some of those silly humans fall in love with me."

"Look," Zeus said proudly. "Look at my creation. I want each of you to give her a gift."

The gods knew they must obey Zeus. They thought about it for a moment; then they each gave Pandora a gift. One god gave her beauty, another gave her charm, and a third gave her a sweet voice.

Zeus gave her a gift too, the most dangerous gift in the world—curiosity. When the gods had given all their gifts, Pandora was the most beautiful woman in the universe. Her hair was like the darkest night. Her eyes sparkled like stars. Her voice was sweeter than golden honey. Zeus knew that no one would be able to resist her.

Zeus filled a golden box with gifts. He shut the box and gave it to Pandora. "Keep this box, but never open it," he ordered her. "Now, come with me. I'm taking you to Earth."

"What is Earth?" Pandora asked, curious.

"Oh, it's a wonderful place," Zeus snickered. "You'll love it, my dear. In fact, you're going to live there."

Zeus and Pandora flew to Earth. They stopped in front of the house where Epimetheus lived. Zeus stood in front of the door, Pandora beside

him. "Epimetheus!" he roared. "I know you're in there. Come out at once."

The door opened a crack. Zeus and Pandora could see one brown eye peeking out. "Oh, no," Epimetheus said. "You can't punish me, Great Zeus. I didn't do anything wrong. You can't chain me up and let some bird rip out my liver. I won't give you the chance."

Zeus chuckled, pretending to be friendly. "Oh, come now, Epimetheus," he said. "I'm not here to punish you; I'm here to make peace. I know you weren't involved in your brother's wretched plot. I just want to show you there's no reason for us not to be friends. In fact, I've brought you a gift. See?" He beckoned to Pandora. She stepped forward, smiling sweetly. Her beauty was like a sunbeam shining across Epimetheus's face.

Epimetheus opened the door. "Who are you?" He gasped, dazzled.

"This is Pandora," Zeus said. "She's never been to Earth before. I thought perhaps you would offer her your hospitality."

Epimetheus almost fell over his own feet as he moved aside. "Please," he said, gesturing toward the house. "Come right in."

"Thank you," Pandora said cheerfully. Still holding the box, she tripped lightly into the house. Epimetheus turned to Zeus.

"Thank... thank you, oh beneficent Zeus," he stammered.

"No, no," Zeus said with a smile. "Thank you." He waved his hand and disappeared.

Now, Epimetheus should have been more cautious. Long ago, Prometheus had warned him never to accept any gift from the gods, especially from Zeus. However, Pandora was so beautiful and so charming that Epimetheus forgot his brother's sage words. Before long, Pandora and Epimetheus fell in love and got married. They lived together in Epimetheus's beautiful mansion, where the golden box always sat on the mantel over the fireplace. They were very happy.

One day, however, Epimetheus had to leave on a short journey. He kissed Pandora good-bye before he left. "I don't like to leave you alone," he said tenderly.

She smiled at him. "I'll be all right," she said, "but come home soon." She stood by the door and waved at Epimetheus as he walked out of sight. Then she went inside. It was a lovely morning, and Pandora wandered through the house, admiring the sunlight as it danced across the floor. One sunbeam came right through the window and landed on the golden box Zeus had given her. The box glowed like a precious gem. Pandora walked up to the box, admiring its beauty. She looked at it for a long time. She remembered Zeus's warning. "Don't ever open it." Unfortunately, her curiosity was stronger than her fear of Zeus.

"I wonder what's inside?" she mused. "It must be something wonderful, to be housed in such a lovely box. Perhaps it's full of exquisite gems, or pearls from Neptune's sea. Maybe it contains rare perfumes or cunning ornaments of gold. Why shouldn't I open it? After all, Zeus gave it to me. It's my property."

With that, Pandora's curiosity won the battle. She took the box off the mantel and set it gently on the floor. She knelt down next to it and placed her hands on the lid. Slowly, very slowly, she lifted the lid. Her eyes were wide, waiting to see the wonderful things inside the gold box.

But there were no gems, no rare essences. Suddenly, a cloud rose out of the open box. It was dark, and it smelled terrible. There were faces in the cloud, evil, wicked faces. They had long teeth, burning eyes, and weeping sores on their faces. They were Disease, Hunger, Sorrow, Greed, and Pain. They swarmed out of the box and out of the house. In a flash, they spread through the world.

"Oh, no!" Pandora cried. She slammed the lid back on the box, but it was too late. The troubles that plague mankind to this day had already escaped.

Pandora slumped to the floor, crying bitterly. "What have I done?" she wept. "What have I done to the world?"

She sat by the box and sobbed for a long time. Then she heard a faint noise. It sounded like a voice. It was coming from inside the golden box.

"Pandora," it cried. "Pandora, let me out."

Pandora shuddered. Who knew what horror still remained in the box? But again, her curiosity was stronger than her fear. She slowly lifted the lid. There, in the bottom of the box, was a shining creature. It looked up at Pandora.

"Don't cry," it said. "My name is Hope. Athena, the goddess of wisdom, put me in the box. She knew that humans would need me in order to survive. Please, lift me out of the box."

Pandora put her hand in and took Hope out of the gold box. It fluttered on her hand for a moment, then flew away. Pandora wiped her tears. She didn't know why, but she felt better now. Everything would be all right. Now you know how evil came into the world. It was due to Pandora and her gift of curiosity. But as long as humans have hope, they will still survive.

Using Context Clues

Skilled readers can often find the meaning of unfamiliar words by studying the way these words are used. This is called *using context clues.* Among the types of context clues are

- **definition.** The writer uses a word and provides its meaning.
- **comparison/contrast.** The word is contrasted to a word with the opposite meaning.
- **examples.** One or more details or examples show the word's meaning.

Directions: Complete the chart below by writing a definition of each **bold** word in the second column. In the last column, identify the type of context clue(s) you used.

Word in Context	Definition	Type of Context Clue(s)
1. "[Zeus] was furious, and when Zeus was **enraged,** nobody was happy."	*enraged* means:	Ⓐ definition Ⓑ comparison/contrast Ⓒ example
2. "Epimetheus should have been more cautious. Long ago, Prometheus had warned him never to accept any gift from the gods, especially from Zeus. [But] Epimetheus forgot his brother's **sage** words."	*sage* means:	Ⓐ definition Ⓑ comparison/contrast Ⓒ example
3. "It must be something wonderful, to be housed in such a lovely box. Perhaps it's full of **exquisite** gems…"	*exquisite* means:	Ⓐ definition Ⓑ comparison/contrast Ⓒ example
4. "Maybe it contains rare perfumes… But there were no gems, no rare **essences**…. [The cloud] smelled terrible."	*essences* means:	Ⓐ definition Ⓑ comparison/contrast Ⓒ example
5. "They were Disease, Hunger, Sorrow, Greed, and Pain….[t]he troubles that **plague** mankind to this day."	*plague* means:	Ⓐ definition Ⓑ comparison/contrast Ⓒ example

Summarizing

Suppose you are asked what "Pandora's Box" is about. One way to explain the story is to *summarize* it, or shorten it into a series of main events.

Directions: The chart below shows one way to summarize "Pandora's Box." Use the right-hand column to answer the questions on the left. An example has been provided.

What problem does Zeus have?	*Zeus, the king of the gods, is angry because Prometheus stole his fire and gave it to the humans.*
What goal does Zeus have?	
How does Zeus attempt to achieve his goal?	
What is the outcome?	
Are there any additional, unexpected outcomes or twists? What are they?	

Point of View

Each of the characters in "Pandora's Box" has a different point of view. Sometimes these different viewpoints result in a conflict between the characters.

Directions: Answer the following questions about the characters' points of view.

1. **Humans**

   a. How does Prometheus view humans? _____

   _____

   b. How does Zeus view humans? _____

   _____

   c. What is the result of these different points of view? _____

   _____

2. **Prometheus**

   a. How does Hermes view Prometheus? _____

   _____

   b. How does Zeus view Prometheus? _____

   _____

   c. What is the result of these different points of view? _____

   _____

3. **The box**

   a. How does Zeus view the box? _____

   _____

   b. How does Pandora view the box? _____

   _____

   c. What is the result of Pandora's view of the box? _____

   _____

GOLD FOR THE CLEVER MAN

A tale from India in Think-Along format
as retold by Frederick Y. Lagbao

As you read: Write your predictions in the space on the right. Feel free to add other comments or questions.

Story

The streets of Cochin were decorated with fragrant and colorful flowers. Women were in their kitchens preparing special dishes for a feast. All the people were dressed in their finest outfits, for it was a special holiday—Vinayaka Chaturthi, or All Fools Day.

One of the most popular events planned for this day was a liars' contest at the palace. The king, who considered himself a talented storyteller, also enjoyed a good tale. And what better way to celebrate All Fools Day than to fool the king! The king was sure he wouldn't have to award any prizes. No one had ever fooled him before.

The townspeople listened excitedly as the king announced the rules and prizes. "The three best liars in the kingdom will each receive a bag of gold," he announced. "The first bag will go to the man who can tell a false tale and make us believe it really happened. The second bag will go to the man who can convince us that a dish he tasted was the most delicious dish of the day. And the third bag will go to the man who can convince us that he is the luckiest man in the kingdom.

"Any man who wishes to enter the contest may do so," the king continued. "The only requirement is that he be good at telling lies." The king paused and glanced at the courtiers gathered around him. "I'm sure none of you are qualified to enter!" he said with a half-smile. All but one of the courtiers shuffled their feet and exchanged nervous looks. No one laughed until he was sure the king was joking.

The one courtier who was not nervous was a young man named Kalloor. He now boldly spoke. "Your majesty, do you remember what the teacher said to King Bali the Great?"

"No," answered the king in a deep voice. "What did he say?"

"He said it was all right for a man to tell falsehoods if he must do so to earn a living."

Other courtiers gasped. It was unheard of to speak directly to the king. But the king just threw back his head and laughed

Your Predictions

Make a prediction: Do you think the king will be fooled this time?

heartily. Then of course, everyone else laughed too. But even as the other courtiers laughed, they cast angry looks at Kalloor. The young man's wit had already made him a favorite with the king, and the others were jealous.

The contest was scheduled to begin when the morning sun peaked in the sky. Many contestants began arriving well before that time, for the king demanded promptness.

By midmorning, several men were already pacing up and down the banquet hall. Some were preparing to tell of finding treasure in a mountain cave or outwitting a goblin. One was rehearsing a tale about a man-eating tiger. Still others planned stories of getting caught in a stampede of wild elephants or bringing home an old lamp with a genie in it. Everyone had an incredible adventure to tell.

Several other men were busy developing stories of delicious foods. They concocted mouthwatering descriptions of coconut chutney, spiced lamb, grilled prawns, chicken curry, sweet carrot pudding, and other heavenly dishes. Some stories were real and some were imagined.

When the sun reached its highest point, the king entered the room. The king nodded regally and sat on a throne placed on a low platform. Royal attendants set before him a table with three bags. The king nodded again, drew his breath, and opened his mouth to declare, "Let the competition begin."

But before the king could speak, an elderly courtier named Dadhich cut him off. "Your Majesty," said Dadhich, "would you mind counting the coins in each bag in full view of the townspeople?"

Since it was a special occasion, the king kindly agreed. With a smile, he pulled out the coins from each bag, one at a time, and carefully counted them. Each bag had exactly 101 coins.

Everyone clapped as the king refilled the last bag. He smiled, nodded, and commenced to declare the contest open. But before he could speak, another voice cut him off.

"Excuse me, your majesty," the voice said. "I wasn't present when the coins were counted. May I see them counted again?"

"Who dares interrupt me again?" the king bellowed, slamming his fist on the table.

"It is I, Kalloor."

Everyone stared at Kalloor as he came forward and stood before the king.

Make a prediction: What role do you predict Kalloor will play in this story?

The king shook his head angrily. "It is enough that everyone here witnessed the counting. They can verify the amount. And besides, you are late! You know how much I despise latecomers. What is your excuse?"

"Well, Your Highness," Kalloor said, "I'm afraid I don't have a very good excuse. I ate too much for breakfast—that's all. I just had to lie down to settle my stomach, and I fell asleep. By the time I awoke, it was almost time for the contest to begin. So I jumped up and rushed out of the house. I tried to run, but you know how hard it is to run on a full stomach."

"Bah, such self-indulgence!" said the king contemptuously. "If there's anything I despise more than tardiness, it's gluttony. Besides, how could you eat so much when you knew there would be a banquet waiting for you here?"

"Sire, my wife had prepared pazha prathaman, and I just couldn't insult her by not eating any."

All this time, the jealous courtiers had been delighted over Kalloor's disgrace. But now it seemed that the king's anger was subsiding. Hoping to make it flare up again, one of the courtiers said to the king, "Bananas, your majesty? How could his wife get bananas? The monsoons came early this year and flooded the crops."

"Yes, Kalloor," said the king, his suspicions aroused. "No one else has bananas. How did yours manage to survive?"

Kalloor nodded. "Your majesty, our tree was brought down from the slopes of the Western Ghats. It was so high there that the floods didn't touch the fields. You see, our daughter, who recently married and moved away, sent that tree to us from her new home. And my wife, who misses our daughter very much, loves that tree. She fusses and prays over it every day. So when it finally bore fruit, she cut the bunch down herself, all eighty-five golden bananas, and made the dish. How could a man fail to show his appreciation for such devotion?"

"You are quite right," agreed the king. "A loving husband does his best to eat his wife's cooking."

"Oh, it was delicious," protested Kalloor. "My wife has her own special recipe. She boils molasses with water to make a rich chestnut-colored syrup. Then she cooks the bananas and adds the syrup and ghee. Next she stirs in fresh milk from coconut meat and lets the mixture simmer. As the sweet aroma fills the house, she fries slices of coconut meat and

Make a prediction.

cumin seeds and adds these to the pudding. What a combination of flavors and textures! It's soft and smooth, yet there's a touch of crispness in each taste. It's sweet and creamy, yet there's a hint of spice to tickle your tongue. In short, my wife's pazha prathaman is a dish fit for a king!"

"If that's the case," said one of the jealous courtiers, "you should have brought it here and presented it to the king, instead of gobbling it all up yourself."

"Yes, yes," cried several others, "your behavior insults the king!"

In the midst of the furor, Kalloor calmly walked to the table and picked up a bag of gold. The king glowered at him. "And what do you think you are doing?" he demanded.

Without batting an eyelash, Kalloor answered, "The story I have just told to explain my tardiness was pure invention. Not a word of it was true; yet you all believed me."

There was stunned silence. Nobody wanted to admit falling into Kalloor's trap, but there was no way to deny it.

The king recovered his good humor. He smiled at the young man and announced that Kalloor rightly deserved the first bag of gold. The audience burst into loud applause.

When the hall was quiet again, Kalloor reached out and took the second bag of gold.

"Now, what is this?" the king asked in surprise. "Why take the second bag?"

Kalloor replied, "Because I also convinced the entire assembly that I had tasted the most delicious dish of this day."

The king let out a roar of laughter. Nobody dared argue, for their mouths had watered as he described the delicious dish. This time the crowd's applause was even louder.

The noise had barely died down when Kalloor stepped up to the table once again and took the third bag of gold. Before anyone could protest, the young man spoke. "Surely, the man who has just won two bags of gold is the luckiest man of all!"

At this, the palace fairly rocked with cheers and laughter. Of course the jealous courtiers were not happy. But everyone else, from the king to the lowliest member of the kingdom, was well pleased with the morning's entertainment. As for the clever Kalloor, he was led home in a parade, tightly clutching his three bags of gold.

Make a prediction: How do you think the king will react to Kalloor's explanation?

Fact and Opinion

A statement of *fact* contains information that can be proved true or false. A statement of *opinion* expresses a personal belief or attitude.

Hint: To recognize an opinion, look for words that show belief or judgment. The signal list below will help you recognize opinions.

should	good	most	believe
should not	best	probably	feel
may	worst	least	think

Directions: Read the pairs of items below and decide whether each statement is a fact or an opinion. Write *Fact* or *Opinion* on the lines provided.

1.

_____ a. Kalloor fools the king and the townspeople.

_____ b. Kalloor is wrong to outsmart the king and townspeople.

_____ c. The king should not have behaved unkindly during the liars' contest.

_____ d. The king disapproves of Kalloor for interrupting him and for arriving late.

_____ e. The liars' contest provides the best way to temporarily undermine the king's power.

_____ f. Each year, townspeople have the opportunity to participate in a contest that undermines the king's power.

2.

> Make this factual statement a statement of opinion.
>
> a. Kalloor's description of his wife's cooking makes everyone's mouth water.

> Make this opinion statement a statement of fact.
>
> b. The courtiers should not have acted as though they were jealous of Kalloor.

Irony

"Gold for the Clever Man" contains several forms of irony. *Irony* occurs when the reality of a thing is different from its appearance. The most common types are explained below.

    a. **Dramatic irony**— occurs when a character believes that something is true, but the audience knows differently.

    b. **Situational irony**— occurs when experience causes a reader to expect one thing, but the opposite takes place.

    c. **Verbal irony**— occurs when a statement is a direct contradiction of reality.

Directions: Read the following examples of irony from the story. Choose the type of irony that is used in the passage.

1. The character Kalloor is young and powerless, yet he fools everyone and wins the liars' contest.

    Ⓐ dramatic irony   Ⓑ situational irony   Ⓒ verbal irony

2. The king says that those who enter the contest must be good at telling lies. Then he glances at the courtiers and says, "I'm sure none of you are qualified to enter!"

    Ⓐ dramatic irony   Ⓑ situational irony   Ⓒ verbal irony

3. The king and the townspeople believe Kalloor arrives late because he has overeaten, but the reader suspects Kalloor is making up the story.

    Ⓐ dramatic irony   Ⓑ situational irony   Ⓒ verbal irony

4. The king holds a liars' contest.

    Ⓐ dramatic irony   Ⓑ situational irony   Ⓒ verbal irony

Summing It Up

Is "Gold for the Clever Man"   Ⓐ a myth   or   Ⓑ a folktale? How do you know?

What question does this story answer or what lesson does it teach?

READING FICTION SELF-CHECK

. . . .

This self-check will help you keep track of your reading progress. The first three lines below each item list strategies that skilled readers often use. Mark how often you use each of these strategies.

1=almost always   2=often   3=sometimes   4=hardly ever

The blank lines are a place where you can add other strategies or feelings you have about reading.

Before I start to read a story, I think about

_____ why I'm reading this selection.

_____ what I expect based on the title.

_____ what I want to learn.

_____ _____

As I read a story, I

_____ try to find a character I can identify with.

_____ think about the relationships among the characters.

_____ think about the narrator's role.

_____ _____

When I come to a word I don't know, I

_____ see if I can guess the meaning from the words around it.

_____ ask someone or look it up.

_____ sound it out.

_____ _____

When a whole sentence doesn't make sense, I

_____ read it again.

_____ read the paragraph before the sentence.

_____ sound out the hardest words.

_____ _____

After I read a story, I

_____ talk to someone else about the piece.

_____ form an opinion about the piece.

_____ think about the themes, or messages, of the piece.

_____ _____

. . . .

Each time you complete this self-check, compare your answers to the answers you came up with the last time you completed the self-check. Then answer these questions.

What is the most important thing you learned from your work with reading skills and strategies?

_____

_____

_____

Describe a time when you used one of these skills or strategies in another class.

_____

_____

_____

What is the most important thing you've learned about reading fiction?

_____

_____

_____

How much better are you at reading now than when you first took this reading self-check?

_____

_____

_____

What tips would you give another student who was having trouble reading a work of fiction?

_____

_____

_____

Reading Poetry

At first glance, poetry might seem hard to understand. That is because poets use language in special ways. They choose words for sound as well as for meaning. And they use literary devices such as rhyme, free verse, rhythm, and figurative language. Sometimes poets play with words and ideas in order to discover new things about a topic. For example, they might compare the purr of a cat to a car engine or a tree to an outstretched hand. Knowing how to read poetry can make understanding it easy.

How to read a poem:

1. Decide what the poem might be about based on the title.

2. Read the poem aloud several times. Listen carefully to the sounds of the words. Think about how the words and the sounds of the poem work together.

3. Try to imagine the objects, actions, or scenes the poet is describing. Form a picture in your mind, if possible.

4. Be aware of punctuation. The end of a line doesn't always mean the end of a sentence. If there's no period, read on to the next line without a pause. If a line ends in a comma, pause briefly before going on.

5. Look at the form, or shape, of the poem. Decide if the way the poem looks adds anything to its meaning.

6. Check to see if the poet uses capitalization, punctuation, or spelling in special ways. If so, what does it add to the meaning of the poem?

7. Based on the details in the poem, try to find the poet's purpose or message. Some poets write to share their ideas or feelings about life. Others simply write to entertain.

As you read through a poem, you might find the Think-Along method helpful to note your reactions to the poem. Each time you read through the poem, add more thoughts to your Think-Along.

THE EAGLE

by Alfred, Lord Tennyson

As you read: See how one reader used the Think-Along method with this poem.

The Eagle
by Alfred, Lord Tennyson

He clasps the crag[1] with crooked hands,   1
Close to the sun in lonely lands,
Ringed with the azure[2] world, he stands.

The wrinkled sea beneath him crawls;
He watches from his mountain walls,   5
And like a thunderbolt he falls.

1. **crag:** a steep, rugged rock or cliff
2. **azure:** sky-blue

Think-Along

The "he" must be the eagle. He's holding onto a cliff with his talons, which resemble crooked hands.

In line 2, "in lonely lands" must mean the eagle is in a place that's pretty deserted—probably a mountaintop because it says he's close to the sun.

"Ringed" in line 3 means surrounded. So the third line says he's surrounded by blue sky. And he's just standing, kind of like a statue.

Okay, this is a new stanza, so maybe something new is going on. Why would the sea be wrinkled? It must be how the waves look to the eagle because he's so high up. I like the image of the sea crawling.

In line 5, the eagle is still watching... I wonder what's coming.

Wow! What an image in line 6! I can just see the eagle go after its prey like lightning coming down from the sky. Quite a contrast to what the eagle was doing earlier.

I think Tennyson probably wrote this poem because he had such respect for eagles.

FOUL SHOT

The familiar nursery rhyme below is considered a traditional poem. Read it aloud.

Mary had a little lamb
Its fleece was white as snow,
And everywhere that Mary went
The lamb was sure to go.

Notice that the poem has a definite rhythm pattern, or beat. The first and third lines have four accented beats (**Ma** ry **had** a **lit** tle **lamb**), while the second and fourth have three (Its **fleece** was **white** as **snow**). Note also that the second and fourth lines rhyme at the end (snow/go) and that all of the lines are basically the same length.

However, not all poetry is traditional. *Free verse* poetry does not always contain a regular rhyme or rhythm. And the length of the lines often depends on the message the poet is trying to get across to the reader.

The arrangement of lines and words, the punctuation, and the number of stanzas, or verses, make up a poem's *form.* You can tell what a poem's form is simply by noticing how the poem appears on the page.

FOUL SHOT

by Edwin A. Hoey

Directions: The first time you read "Foul Shot," try to keep the "How to Read a Poem" tips in mind.

As you read: Each time you reread the poem, note your reactions in the Think-Along column. Pay close attention to the form of the poem. Try to note how the form is related to the meaning.

Foul Shot

Think-Along

by Edwin A. Hoey

With two 60's stuck on the scoreboard
And two seconds hanging on the clock,
The solemn boy in the center of eyes,
Squeezed by silence,
Seeks out the line with his feet,   5
Soothes his hands along his uniform,
Gently drums the ball against the floor,
Then measures the waiting net,
Raises the ball on his right hand,
Balances it with his left,   10
Calms it with fingertips,
Breathes,
Crouches,
Waits,
And then through a stretching of stillness,   15
Nudges it upward.

The ball slides up and out.
Lands,
Leans,
Wobbles,   20
Wavers,
Hesitates,
Exasperates,
Plays it coy
Until every face begs with unsounding screams— 25
And then
                And then,
                            And then,
Right before ROAR-UP,
Dives down and through.   30

FOUL SHOT

Building Suspense

Suspense is the tension created when the author withholds information from the reader. Suspense keeps the reader's interest and causes the reader to want to read on. The activity below will help you determine the way the poet creates suspense.

Directions: The questions below examine the ways the poet uses line length and punctuation in "Foul Shot" to create suspense. As you answer items 1–5, refer to your Think-Along notes for help.

1. Some of the most suspenseful lines in "Foul Shot" are lines 18–24. What do these lines have in common? How does line length help create suspense?

_____

_____

_____

2. What is different about the pattern of lines 26–28? How might these lines reflect the action in the poem? (Hint: Picture the ball in your mind as you reread these lines.)

_____

_____

3. A comma signals a short pause. Reread "Foul Shot." How does the poet's use of commas add to the suspense of the poem?

_____

_____

4. A dash (—) indicates a pause that is stronger than a comma but not as strong as a period. Why do you think the poet chose to use a dash rather than a comma or a period at the end of line 25?

_____

_____

5. A period indicates a complete thought. Count the number of periods in "Foul Shot." How does the poet use periods to divide the poem?

_____

_____

Personification

Personification is the technique of giving human qualities to something that is not human. For example, "The old car **coughed** and **wheezed** as it **struggled** to climb the steep road."

Directions: Answer the following questions to get a better understanding of personification.

1. What is personified in "Foul Shot"?

    Ⓐ the crowd

    Ⓑ the net

    Ⓒ the ball

2. What lines from the poem support your answer to the previous question?

    Ⓐ With two 60's stuck on the scoreboard
    And two seconds hanging on the clock

    Ⓑ Hesitates,
    Exasperates,
    Plays it coy

    Ⓒ And then
    And then,
    And then,
    Right before ROAR-UP

3. How does the use of personification add to the suspense of the poem?

    _____

    _____

Your Turn

Assume that the boy missed the shot. Rewrite the last line of the poem and add any additional lines you think are necessary to complete the new ending.

_____

_____

_____

_____

_____

_____

THE SEA

by James Reeves

As you read: People are sometimes described as having more than one "side." In other words, their personalities often change, depending on the situation. How many "sides" might the sea have? What are they? Consider these questions as you read the following poem.

. . . .

The Sea
by James Reeves

The sea is a hungry dog,
Giant and gray.
He rolls on the beach all day.
With his clashing teeth and shaggy jaws
Hour upon hour he gnaws   5
The rumbling, tumbling stones,
And "Bones, bones, bones, bones!"
The giant sea-dog moans,
Licking his greasy paws.

And when the night wind roars   10
And the moon rocks in the stormy cloud,
He bounds to his feet and snuffs and sniffs,
Shaking his wet sides over the cliffs,
And howls and hollos long and loud.

But on quiet days in May or June,   15
When even the grasses on the dune
Play no more their reedy tune,
With his head between his paws
He lies on the sandy shores,
So quiet, so quiet, he scarcely snores.   20

Comparisons

A *simile* is a comparison that uses the word *like* or *as.* "Tom runs like the wind" is a simile.

A *metaphor* is a comparison that does not use *like* or *as.* The first line of "The Sea" is a metaphor because it says that the sea *is* a hungry dog. The poet then *extends* this metaphor. That is, he goes on to show several dog-like qualities that the sea possesses.

Poets use metaphors and similes to help their readers picture what is happening in a poem. They compare an event, idea, or thing to something the reader is already familiar with. Everyone has probably seen a hungry dog. Therefore, it's easy for most readers to picture the sea the way the poet describes it.

Directions: Answer the following questions to gain a better understanding of "The Sea."

Stanza 1

1. Look back at "The Sea." List three dog-like qualities the sea has in the first stanza, or verse.

_____

_____

_____

2. What picture do you get of the sea after reading the first stanza?

_____

_____

_____

3. Which word best describes the side of the sea's personality as shown in the first stanza?

    Ⓐ unhappy   Ⓒ furious

    Ⓑ restless   Ⓓ playful

Stanza 2

4. What three dog-like qualities does the sea have in the second stanza?

_____

_____

_____

5. What picture do you get of the sea after reading the second stanza?

_____

_____

_____

6. Which word best describes the side of the sea's personality as shown in stanza 2?

Ⓐ lonely   Ⓒ evil

Ⓑ angry   Ⓓ frightened

Stanza 3

7. What three dog-like qualities is the sea given in the third stanza?

_____

_____

_____

8. What picture do you get of the sea after reading the third stanza?

_____

_____

_____

9. Which word best describes the side of the sea's personality as shown in stanza 3?

Ⓐ crafty   Ⓒ sad

Ⓑ peaceful   Ⓓ gloomy

10. Do you think a dog is an appropriate choice to show the different sides of the sea? Why or why not? What other animals would work well to show the different sides of the sea?

_____

_____

_____

CATALOG

by Rosalie Moore

As you read: Based on the picture and the title, what do you expect from this poem?

· ·

Catalog

by Rosalie Moore

Cats sleep fat and walk thin.
Cats, when they sleep, slump;
When they wake, pull in—
And where the plump's been
There's skin.   5
Cats walk thin.

Cats wait in a lump,
Jump in a streak.
Cats, when they jump, are sleek
As a grape slipping its skin—   10
They have technique.
Oh, cats don't creak.
They sneak.

Cats sleep fat.
They spread comfort beneath them   15
Like a good mat,
As if they picked the place
And then sat.
You walk around one
As if he were the City Hall   20
After that.

If male,
A cat is apt to sing on a major scale:
This concert is for everybody, this
Is wholesale.   25
For a baton, he wields a tail.
(He is also found,
When happy, to resound
With an enclosed and private sound.)

A cat condenses.   30
He pulls in his tail to go under bridges,
And himself to go under fences.
Cats fit
In any size box or kit;
And if a large pumpkin grew under one, 35
He could arch over it.

When everyone else is just ready to go out,
The cat is just ready to come in.
He's not where he's been.
Cats sleep fat and walk thin.   40

Alliteration

Alliteration is the repetition of consonant sounds. Usually, but not always, alliteration occurs at the beginning of words. "Rock and roll" and "calm, cool, and collected" are examples of alliteration. Alliteration can set the mood of a poem by giving words a musical quality. For example, several words in a row starting with the letter *m* can convey a quiet, calm mood. Alliteration also adds rhythm to writing. And it draws attention to certain words. Words that begin with the same consonant sound naturally stand out from the others.

Directions: Answer the questions below to understand why alliteration is popular with poets.

---

1. Look at line 2 from "Catalog" below.

   Cats, when they sleep, slump.

   Line 2 contains alliteration. Both "sleep" and "slump" begin with the letter *s*. Find another example of alliteration in the poem that uses the letter *s*. Write the example below and underline the *s* sounds.

   _____

   _____

2. Besides beginning many words, the *s* sound is used frequently within words in this poem. Notice the repetition of the *s* sound in lines 30 and 31 below.

   A cat condenses.
   He pulls in his tail to go under bridges,
   And himself to go under fences.

   Find another example of the repetition of the *s* sound within words in "Catalog." Write it on the lines below.

   _____

   _____

3. Why might the poet have chosen to alliterate the *s* sound in a poem about cats?

   _____

   _____

Figurative Language

Figurative language helps paint pictures in a reader's mind. Two of the most common types of figurative language are similes and metaphors.

A *simile* is a comparison that uses the word *like* or *as.* "The children stood as still as statues" is an example of a simile. A *metaphor* is a comparison that does not use *like* or *as.* Instead it might indicate that two things are equal. "Leon was a raging bull on the football field" is a

metaphor. A metaphor can also make a comparison by suggesting that one thing is like another. For example, "Suddenly she erupted in anger, spitting out her bitter remarks at the guests." The words *erupted* and *spitting out* suggest a comparison between the woman and a volcano.

Directions: To better understand the poem "Catalog," answer the following questions.

1. Lines 9–10 in "Catalog" contain a simile. Reread these lines. Then draw or describe the picture the simile creates in your mind.

Draw	Describe
	_____
	_____
	_____

2. Lines 14–21 contain several similes. Reread the third stanza. Then draw or describe the overall picture the similes create in your mind.

Draw	Describe
	_____
	_____
	_____

3. Lines 22–26 contain metaphors. Reread the fourth stanza of "Catalog." Then draw or describe the overall picture the metaphors create in your mind.

Draw	Describe
	_____
	_____
	_____

CATALOG

Contrasts

Part of the fun of "Catalog" is the contrasting words the poet uses to describe cats. For example, in the first line, "Cats sleep fat and walk thin," "fat" is the opposite of "thin." And, to some extent, "sleep" is the opposite of "walk," or being up and around. This activity will help you appreciate the contrasts in "Catalog."

Directions: Listed below are several words that the poet combines with opposite words in the poem. Fill in the blanks with the opposite words from the poem (lines 1–13). Then answer the questions that follow.

Word	Opposite
fat	thin
sleep	walk
wake	
slump	
skin	
jump	
lump	
sneak	

1. Why do you think the poet uses contrasting images to describe cats?

_____

_____

2. What is the main idea of this poem?

Ⓐ Cats seek comfort above all else.

Ⓑ Cats, like humans, change with their moods.

Ⓒ Most cats are overweight.

Ⓓ Cats have little need for human care.

READING POETRY SELF-CHECK

. . . .

This self-check will help you keep track of your reading progress. The first three lines below each item list strategies that skilled readers often use. Mark how often you use each of these strategies.

1=almost always   2=often   3=sometimes   4=hardly ever

The blank lines are a place where you can add other strategies or feelings you have about reading poetry.

Before I start to read a poem, I think about

_____ why I'm reading this poem.

_____ what I expect based on the title.

_____ what I want to learn.

_____ _____

As I read poetry, I

_____ try to see how the poem's form, or shape, relates to its meaning.

_____ think about how the words and sounds work together to create meaning.

_____ try to imagine the objects, actions, or feelings the poet is describing.

_____ _____

When I come to a word in a poem I don't know, I

_____ check to see if it is explained in a footnote at the bottom of the page.

_____ see if I can guess what the word means, or I look it up.

_____ sound out the word and try to guess the meaning from any prefixes or suffixes, or from the root word.

When I don't understand an image or a description in a poem, I

_____ see if anything in the stanza helps me figure it out.

_____ refer back to the title for clues.

_____ reread the image or description and try to relate it to my own experience.

_____ _____

After I've read the poem once, I

_____ reread the poem until I find a meaning that makes sense to me.

_____ reflect on the poet's message.

_____ form an opinion on the worthiness of the poem.

_____ _____

What is the most important thing you've learned about reading poetry?

_____

_____

_____

What tips would you give another student who was having trouble reading poetry?

_____

_____

_____

Reading for Information

Readers take different approaches to informational pieces. You might

- read what you enjoy or what interests you, whether it's *The Guinness Book of World Records* or real-life adventures

- read what you need
  —to fulfill an assignment
  —to complete a task
  —to answer your question(s)

Your reason for reading will shape the questions you ask as you read. Here are one reader's questions about the passage below. What other questions might you ask?

Passage

During the summer of 1966, Gerry and Parker were two typical eleven-year-old kids fishing for minnows along the banks of Lake Louise in Florida, something they did often. But on this day something so unexpected and terrible happened that they never forgot it for as long as they lived.

Lake Louise is a quiet lake and one that is normally safe, so they were not concerned about any danger. There was nothing to worry about. The sun was high in the sky and the day was warm. Everything was right with the world.

It was then that it happened. Gerry saw something floating offshore. *It might only be a piece of bark, broken off from a tree,* she thought. *But it might also be a wallet. It might be valuable.*

Wading into the water, she reached out for the object—

Think-Along

Is this a true story? It could be because of specific details like the date and location of the lake.

"Unexpected and terrible…"—what's going to happen?

I'm getting a feel for how this is organized —it's like a story.

Everything's going perfectly—that means trouble's coming.

I remember reading that crocodiles sometimes look like logs. And they're in Florida, where crocodiles live. Watch out, Gerry!

ATTACK OF THE GATOR

from *True Fright: Trapped Beneath the Ice! and Other True Stories Scarier Than Fiction*
by Ted Pedersen

Reason to read: Decide whether this true story is scarier than fiction.

As you read: Write or draw your thoughts about what's happening in the Think-Along column. (See the model on pages 7–8.) You might want to make a comment every time you guess what's happening next or have a question. You should make at least four comments.

Passage

During the summer of 1966, Gerry and Parker were two typical eleven-year-old kids fishing for minnows along the banks of Lake Louise in Florida, something they did often. But on this day something so unexpected and terrible happened that they never forgot it for as long as they lived.

Lake Louise is a quiet lake and one that is normally safe, so they were not concerned about any danger. There was nothing to worry about. The sun was high in the sky and the day was warm. Everything was right with the world.

It was then that it happened. Gerry saw something floating off-shore. *It might only be a piece of bark, broken off from a tree,* she thought. *But it might also be a wallet. It might be valuable.* Wading into the water, she reached out for the object—

Suddenly something grabbed her arm.

There was a sharp sensation of pain that surged through her whole body.

For an instant she was afraid to look, then she glanced down, and nearly fainted with fear: a huge, hideous-looking monster with rows of razor sharp teeth and terrifying eyes stared up at her malevolently from beneath the water. An alligator!

The creature had ahold of her arm, and even through her long shirt, she saw blood dripping where the gator's teeth had broken the skin.

Think-Along

60

"Help! Parker!" Gerry screamed.

Parker, who was a dozen feet away, had his back turned, so he did not see the attack. Now he turned in response to Gerry's scream and saw the huge gator dragging his friend out into the lake.

Gerry screamed again. Parker stood there stock-still for a long moment. This couldn't be happening, not in Lake Louise.

But it was. And there were no adults around to help them. They were on their own. *He was on his own.* He was Gerry's only hope.

Gerry continued to struggle with the gator, but it was no use. The creature was twice her size. Her efforts were futile against its massive strength.

As the gator pulled Gerry out into the lake, her feet were starting to slip on the soft, wet sand. She remembered a story she had once read about how a wolf caught in a bear trap might gnaw off its own leg to escape. She looked at her arm, held fast in the gator's great mouth, and thought in horror that losing her arm might be the only way she could escape.

On the other hand, she did not want to die. Not now, not on this beautiful day in the warm sun.

Suddenly there was splashing and Parker was there beside her.

"Parker! It won't let go!" Gerry cried.

Parker grabbed Gerry's other arm and pulled. It was a nightmare tug-of-war between him and the gator—with Gerry stretched between them.

This wasn't going to work. Parker let go of Gerry, and without thinking of how dangerous it was, he stepped deeper into the water and pounded on the gator's head with both fists, as hard as he could.

ATTACK OF THE GATOR

That seemed to have no effect. Then suddenly the gator turned and lunged at him. The gator snapped viciously, and Parker leaped back. The jaws were just inches from his face, and Parker could feel its hot breath, smell its rancid odor that reminded him of dead things that had decayed.

But the gator had let loose of Gerry.

Parker recovered quickly and pulled Gerry out of the water before the gator could grab her again. Stumbling and crawling, the two children made their way up onto the bank of the lake.

Exhausted, they lay for a long moment in the grass. The terrible ordeal was over. They were safe.

But then Parker looked behind him and saw that the alligator had crawled onto the shore and was now moving toward them. Parker had always thought that gators were slow and clumsy on land, but this one was coming at them with surprising speed.

"We have to get outta here!" Parker cried to Gerry.

"My arm hurts…can't move…" she mumbled.

"You have to. The gator's comin'!"

Parker pulled Gerry to her feet. By accident, he grabbed her injured arm, and she yelled in pain. But he had to ignore the hurt he caused her or they'd both be gator bait.

Now they ran through the grass as the gator pursued them.

Parker stumbled and they both fell. Too scared to look behind him, afraid to see how close the gator was, Parker scrambled to his feet and he and Gerry continued to run.

They were almost to the spot where they had left their bicycles when Parker dared to turn and look.

The gator was only a few feet behind them!

Parker was shocked. What did the creature want?

It wanted them, of course, and it could outrun them on land. They would tire and drop long before it did.

Their bicycles were their only hope.

But Gerry was only half conscious from the pain and fear. There was no way she could ride her bike. It was up to him.

Parker lifted his bicycle upright and pushed Gerry up and over the bar in front of the seat. He was glad that it was his bike and not hers. There was no bar on a girl's bike to balance her.

She almost fell off at first, but then she managed to hang on. Parker started to get on the bike, but then he realized that the gator was snapping at his heels. He shoved the bicycle along for several feet with Gerry hanging on, the gator in hot pursuit.

Finally, there was enough space between him and the gator that Parker was able to climb onto the bicycle.

The bicycle teetered, and Parker had the terrible thought that it would tip over and they would be devoured by the monster, but after a few frantic seconds, he was able to balance himself and Gerry. He began to pedal as hard and fast as he had ever done.

All the way from the lake to the road, he never once looked behind him. But when he finally reached the road, he summoned up the courage to turn around. He saw no sign of the predator. It was with a great sigh of relief that he realized they had outrun the gator.

Parker flagged down a car, and the driver took them to the local hospital, where Gerry's arm was treated. It was a bad gash and took eighteen stitches to close, but she was going to be all right—thanks to her friend's bravery.

Parker didn't feel very brave, though. He was as scared as he had ever been in his life, but Gerry was his friend and he knew that she would have done the same for him.

Later, when the authorities started a search for the gator, they were able to locate its tracks, but the gator itself had vanished back into the lake. They searched the lake by boat for the next three days, but wherever the gator had come from, it seemed to have returned.

Once more Lake Louise was safe.

But it was going to be a long time before Parker and Gerry returned to the lake to fish—if ever.

Spine-Tingling Words

The author wanted this true story to be "scarier than fiction." This purpose influenced his choice of words. The two sentences below describe the same event. However, one statement is *neutral*; it simply states the facts without using words that create strong emotion. The other is taken from the selection. Notice that the author isn't satisfied with the neutral word *alligator*. Instead, he tries to create fear by describing a huge monster with an evil stare.

In the activity below you get to try your hand at using neutral and emotional words.

Directions: Read the example. Then finish the chart below. In the Scary column, add emotional words and scary details from the selection. In the Neutral column, reword the Scary statement so it gives only the facts. If you don't know the meaning of a word like *malevolently*, you can guess the meaning or use a dictionary.

example

Neutral	Scary
An alligator looked up at her from beneath the water.	A huge, hideous-looking monster with rows of razor sharp teeth and terrifying eyes stared up at her malevolently from beneath the water.

Neutral	Scary
1. Gerry could not free herself from the gator.	
2.	It was a nightmare tug-of-war between Parker and the gator—with Gerry stretched between them.
3. Parker could feel and smell the gator's breath.	
4.	Parker had the terrible thought that…they would be devoured by the monster.
5.	He saw no sign of the predator.

Summarizing

Suppose you are writing a report about how people make decisions in emergencies. You want to use Parker's rescue as one of your examples. Here is one way you might summarize the decisions Parker made during the rescue. The column on the left identifies important information. The sentences on the right show a concise, or short, way to state that information.

Directions: Complete the summary, using the hints below.

Hints for Summarizing

- Look for topic sentences. If you find the main idea of a paragraph stated in one sentence, state the idea in your own words. If the author did not use a topic sentence, make one up.

- Include only the most important information in your summary. Information in topic sentences is usually important. (If everything seems important, include only what you would tell a friend who asked you what this piece is about.)

- Shorten and combine related paragraphs. Some paragraphs simply explain other paragraphs.

- Polish your summary. Your first summary will probably sound choppy. Look for places where you need to add connecting words, such as *and, because, next,* or *however.*

Situation	An alligator grabs an eleven-year-old girl who is fishing by a Florida lake and starts dragging her into the water.
Parker's first reaction	At first, her friend Parker can't believe it's happening.
Parker's first decision	Then
Parker's other decisions	
Outcome	

A SUSPICIOUS PACKAGE

from At Risk: Bomb Squads & SWAT Teams
by Jean Dick

Reason to read: Find out about a risky job.
As you read: Look for the facts behind the story.

Sergeant Jordan of the 85th Precinct's bomb squad had just finished his paperwork and was sitting down for a cup of coffee when the telephone rang.

"I'm calling from a gas station near County Road 45 and Highway 1," the voice over the phone said. "There's a suspicious package in the field where I've been working. It's ticking. Can you come right away?"

"I'll be right there," said Jordan. He remembered that a new powerline was being built in that area. There had been protests and threats. This could be the real thing. In fact, a threat is always treated as the real thing until proven otherwise.

Sergeant Jordan called his partner, Officer Phillips. They met at the bomb truck and in minutes the bomb squad was in motion. At the same time police squad cars rushed to the scene and evacuated the area.

When Officers Jordan and Phillips arrived, the area was clear. They parked their truck a safe distance away and put on the 49-pound bomb suits that shield their bodies. Now they were ready to move in for a closer look at the package. They heard steady ticking coming from the package and moved quickly back to the truck.

"Should we jar it?" Phillips asked. The officers can tell if a package will explode at a touch by using a remote control device.

"How about moving it with the bomb trailer?" suggested Jordan.

"No, the area is clear, and no one will be hurt if the bomb goes off right now. We don't need to move it."

"Maybe we should defuse it with a water cannon." This stream of water under high pressure can separate the power source from the blasting cap.

"Let's detonate," decided Phillips. "The area is clear. There's no danger to anything or anybody."

Jordan agreed. The bomb squad uses remote control to set off bombs. They prepared their equipment and called out the warning:

"Fire in the hole! Fire in the hole! Fire in the hole!"

They then fired the "hell box" and a huge explosion filled the air. The sky turned grey with dirt and the ground shook. The officers made the right decision. The bomb was real. It was safely detonated, and no one was hurt. When a bomb is defused in this way, it is called a "high order detonation."

The bomb squad drove back to headquarters to write a report.

Using Context Clues

Everyone encounters new words while reading. Sometimes the only thing to do is to stop and look them up in the dictionary. But skilled readers are often able to find the meaning of new words by examining how they are used in the text. This is called *using context clues*.

Directions: Use the clues below to determine the meaning of the words in **bold** type. If you need more clues, reread the section of the story in which the bold-faced word appears. Then choose the answer that best matches the meaning of the word. (A sample activity is done for you.)

sample "There's a **suspicious package** in the field where I've been working."

Clue: "It's ticking."
Additional clues: The caller reported the package to the bomb squad. Sergeant Jordan concluded that this could be the real thing.

- Ⓐ package that arrives unexpectedly
- ● package that might be dangerous
- Ⓒ package given as a gift
- Ⓓ package that came unwrapped

1. At the same time, police squad cars rushed to the scene and **evacuated** the area.

    Clue: Officer Phillips says the area is clear; no one will be hurt if the bomb explodes.

    - Ⓐ surrounded
    - Ⓑ searched
    - Ⓒ blocked off
    - Ⓓ cleared

2. "Maybe we should defuse it with a **water cannon.**"

    Clue: This stream of water under high pressure can separate the power source from the blasting cap.

    - Ⓐ weapon designed for use on ships
    - Ⓑ extra-large water pistol
    - Ⓒ device that shoots a stream of water
    - Ⓓ sprinker system

3. "Let's **detonate,**" decided Phillips.

    Clue: The bomb squad uses remote control to set off bombs....When a bomb is defused in this way, it is called a "high order detonation."

    - Ⓐ blow up
    - Ⓑ run away
    - Ⓒ check out
    - Ⓓ sound out

A SUSPICIOUS PACKAGE

Reading for Information

This description of how a bomb squad works is based on facts. The author chose to present the facts as a story. Rather than listing the steps in a procedure, she describes an incident in which two officers follow the procedure.

Directions: Answer the questions below to find the facts behind the story.

1. Jean Dick describes what members of the bomb squad do when they arrive at the scene. Identify two ways the officers protect themselves when they approach a bomb.

    a. _____

    b. _____

2. The author could have said, "The officers have four ways to handle bombs." Instead, she wrote a dialogue in which the officers chose one of the four options. List the four ways the bomb squad handles bombs.

    a. _____

    b. _____

    c. _____

    d. _____

3. The author concludes that "the officers made the right decision." List two factors that Officers Jordan and Phillips considered as they made that decision.

    a. _____

    _____

    b. _____

    _____

Organizing Information

Suppose that you're preparing an oral report about how bomb threats are handled. Your teacher has suggested that you speak from an outline.

An *outline* arranges ideas in their order of importance. The most important ideas are labeled with Roman numerals (I, II, III, etc.). The most important supporting ideas are labeled with capital letters (A, B, C, etc.).

Sometimes these supporting ideas are explained with details or examples, which are labeled with Arabic numerals (1, 2, 3, etc.).

Directions: Use the information in the right-hand column to complete the outline below. (Hint: The ideas in the outline are arranged in the same order as in the article. If you need help, go back to the article.)

How the Bomb Squad Handles Bombs

Outline

I.   Respond to a call

   A. Treat each potential bomb as the real thing

   B. _____

   C. Clear the area

II. _____

   A. Check out the package

      1. _____

      2. _____

   B. _____

      1. Jar it

      2. _____

      3. _____

      4. _____

   C. _____

III. _____

Information

Important Ideas (Roman numerals)

~~Respond to a call~~

Write a report on the incident

Deal with the bomb

Supporting Ideas (capital letters)

~~Treat each potential bomb as the real thing~~

~~Clear the area~~

~~Check out the package~~

Discuss ways to handle the bomb

Alert the bomb squad

Explode the bomb

Details and Examples (Arabic numerals)

~~Jar it~~

Move it with a bomb trailer

Put on protective gear

Defuse it with a water cannon

Examine the package

Detonate it by remote control

MY FOUR-LEGGED PARTNER IN HEALING

from *Love, Miracles, and Animal Healing*
by Allen M. Schoen, D.V.M., and Pam Proctor

Reason to read: Find out how this four-legged partner helps a veterinarian.
As you read: Notice what makes this four-legged partner special.

When I first saw the sick, homeless golden retriever, she had the worst case of heartworm disease I had ever seen. Thousands of microfilaria, or baby worms, had moved into her heart tissue.

From the coarse sound of her breathing I suspected she would die of heart failure. But looking into her pleading eyes, I knew I couldn't abandon her. "If you make it," I promised, "I'll keep you."

A friend of mine had found the dog not far from Peterborough, N.H., where I had my first job as a veterinarian. There were no identification tags, not even a collar to suggest that someone had once loved and cared for her. I was hooked the minute I saw her, though, and named her Megan.

She was about four years old, and although her dark gold coat was dull and dry, I could tell she had once been a beauty. Now she just looked haggard. Her gums were pale, and her hacking cough signaled the severity of her condition.

Twice a day for the next three days, I injected a derivative of arsenic into Megan's bloodstream through a catheter in her right front leg. The poison would slowly break down and kill the worms that were clogging her heart. Megan must have

sensed I was trying to help her. Never once did she flinch from the needle. Instead she'd hold out her paw so I could insert the I.V.

For the next month I kept Megan in a cage at the animal hospital, an old barn filled with recovering patients. At night I brought her home to my cabin, where she would curl up on a blanket in front of the wood stove.

After about two months her cough had gone, there was a brightness to her eyes, and her coat had the beginnings of a healthy sheen. A blood test revealed that she was cured. As I leaned over to hug her, I must have communicated the joy I felt because Megan let out a couple of boisterous barks, wagged her tail and slobbered my face with kisses.

From that moment on she came alive, and the sweetness and warmth that had drawn me to her in the first place took on a new dimension. She seemed to possess a special gift for reaching out to others, an unlimited capacity to love.

My first glimpse of it came the night a farmer brought in a lamb that had been attacked by a pack of wild dogs. The lamb was covered with puncture wounds from the dogs' teeth. I quickly administered an electrolyte solution to treat her for shock. After a half-hour she began to improve, but I still didn't think she would make it through the night. I brought her home and let her sleep in front of the wood stove so I could check on her.

But I never got the chance to play nurse. Megan immediately took over, gently licking and nuzzling the lamb. She responded to Megan's attentions with a wan little bleat. Megan paused to listen to the *baaaa*, then resumed her ministrations. When she had finished, she nestled alongside the lamb for the night.

Early the next morning I was roused by Megan. Thinking the worst, I jumped out of bed and ran into the living room. There, standing before me on sturdy legs, was the lamb. Right alongside, like a proud mother, was Megan, her tail wagging wildly.

I began to look at Megan as a partner in healing. Often when I had to go to the animal hospital for an emergency, I would take her with me and let her roam the wards to see "her" patients. I would watch incredulously as she went from cage to cage, licking the animals and caressing them. It didn't matter whether the creature was a dog, a cat or a ferret. Her approach was always the same: love them, lick them and sometimes even lie down with them.

One time a pregnant cat was rushed to the hospital screeching in pain. The cat, a Maine coon, had delivered one kitten at home, but another was stuck in the birth canal. I did an emergency Cesarean section and breathed a sigh of relief. Two little gray balls of wet fur were still alive.

I carefully plucked the kittens from the womb and handed them to the owner. The kittens cried and cried. Their loud mews summoned Megan to action. She rushed to the kittens' box and started licking their fuzzy bodies. I could read the owner's thoughts: *would the dog harm the kittens as they lay weak and blind?* Then the look of concern softened. "She's like a surrogate mother!" the owner said in wonder.

By the time the new mother awakened from the anesthesia, she was well enough to nurse her kittens. Megan willingly stepped aside, her tail wagging in approval as she watched.

Skeptics might argue that Megan's nursing instincts came from her breeding as a golden retriever. But I was convinced that Megan radiated a special aura of acceptance that even broke through to the more unlovable creatures.

This was never more apparent than the day a ferret, emaciated and sick with liver disease, was brought to me. Ferrets can make wonderful pets, but they are also prone to nipping and are notoriously smelly because of glandular secretions. This

one's owner had made the mistake of putting him in mothballs to get rid of the odor. But mothballs are highly toxic, and the fumes started destroying the ferret's liver. His belly was yellow, his gums were bleeding, and he had lost so much weight that he was only an inch in diameter.

I administered fluids beneath the skin to flush the poison from his system, and after a few days he began to respond. It was then that Megan jumped in with her treatment.

Every day she would playfully push the ferret to and fro with her snout. Even when he grabbed her nose in his tiny teeth, Megan didn't flinch or retaliate. She just waited patiently until he let go and then nuzzled him softly with her nose. After a week the ferret was completely well. Once again Megan had worked her magic.

A short time later my fiancée, Barbara, and I let Megan attend our wedding. During the ceremony she parked herself between us—and then promptly fell asleep.

One spring day when Megan was in the back yard chasing birds, she tripped ever so slightly. A week later I caught her limping almost imperceptibly on her right front leg.

X-rays of the leg confirmed my worst fears: bone cancer. I ruled out the traditional treatment of radiation and chemotherapy, along with amputation to arrest the spread of the disease. Megan was fourteen, and I couldn't put her through such suffering.

That night Barbara and I cried softly together and told Megan how much we loved her. In the coming weeks we tried to make her as comfortable as we could with home-cooked meals, natural painkillers and anti-inflammatory agents. But the truth was we didn't need to do anything for Megan. Just as she had nursed others, she quite naturally took care of herself.

As her cancer progressed, she started slowing down on our walks. If she grew tired, she'd stop to sniff some bushes or watch a butterfly. Soon our strolls were nothing more than a slow meander up the driveway. While the tumor grew, Megan sought out a natural spring in back of our house, where she would soak her leg in the mud. Mud packs are used in many cultures to heal inflammation associated with some types of cancer. No one urged Megan toward this healing method. She just knew.

Four months passed from the day I first detected the tumor, and little by little Megan weakened. One day her body was so leaden that she couldn't lift her head. I knelt and looked into her eyes. "Old gal," I said gently, "this is it, isn't it?"

My wife and I sat hugging her for a while. Then I went to get a hypodermic needle. When I returned, I sat immobile, not wanting to face the inevitable. Megan seemed to lift her right paw ever so slightly to receive the injection. Within seconds it was over. While Barbara cradled her head, Megan let out a deep sigh and died.

In the ten years I had Megan, she taught me that the elemental bonds of nature are as powerful as anything the scientific establishment has to offer—and more mysterious. In those bonds are the strands of love, of kindness, of physical and spiritual healing. They are the strands of life itself.

Reading for Detail

The author knew that Megan was special as soon as he saw her. But his readers will never meet this golden retriever. How can the author make us believe that Megan is a unique and wonderful dog?

One way is by using descriptive detail to show Megan's special characteristics.

Directions: Answer the questions below by choosing the detail that best describes Megan.

1. The author was first drawn to Megan by the dog's

    Ⓐ beautiful golden coat.

    Ⓑ boundless energy.

    Ⓒ expressive eyes.

2. Megan's reaction to a wounded lamb showed that she

    Ⓐ feared the unknown.

    Ⓑ reached out to others in love.

    Ⓒ was part wolf.

3. Megan reacted to the doctor's patients

    Ⓐ with jealousy.

    Ⓑ as if they were her patients.

    Ⓒ by ignoring them.

4. Megan's response to a ferret showed her ability to

    Ⓐ do acrobatic tricks.

    Ⓑ adapt to a new playmate.

    Ⓒ accept a creature that others consider unlovable.

5. This dog had an instinctive knowledge of how to

    Ⓐ care for herself and other animals.

    Ⓑ get along with other dogs.

    Ⓒ survive in the wild.

Using Context Clues

Everyone encounters new words while reading. Sometimes the only thing to do is to stop and look them up in the dictionary. But skilled readers are often able to find the meaning of new words by examining how they are used in the text. This is called *using context clues*.

Directions: Write a possible meaning for each **bold** word below.

1. …She had the worst case of **heartworm** disease I had ever seen.

   Clue: Thousands of microfilaria, or baby worms, had moved into her heart tissue. [The drug would] kill the worms that were clogging her heart.

   Possible meaning:_____

   _____

   Additional clue(s) that helped you identify the meaning: _____

   _____

2. "She's like a **surrogate** mother."

   Clue: [The mother cat] was well enough to nurse her kittens. Megan willingly stepped aside.

   Possible meaning:_____

   _____

   Additional clue(s) that helped you identify the meaning: _____

   _____

3. Even when [the ferret] grabbed her nose in his tiny teeth, Megan didn't flinch or **retaliate.**

   Clue: She just waited patiently until he let go.

   Possible meaning:_____

   _____

   Additional clue(s) that helped you identify the meaning: _____

   _____

4. Soon our strolls were nothing but a slow **meander** up the driveway.

   Clue: …She started slowing down on our walks.

   Possible meaning:_____

   _____

   Additional clue(s) that helped you identify the meaning: _____

   _____

Proof by Example

The author concludes that "the elemental bonds of nature are as powerful as anything the scientific establishment has to offer." Someone who hadn't read the entire piece might wonder "What does that mean?"

Asking that question is a good strategy to use when you read a *generality*—a broad statement that can apply to many different things. Authors who write generalities often help readers understand them by providing several specific examples.

Directions: The chart below shows three examples of animal patients that Megan and the doctor treated. Complete the chart. Then compare the results that Megan and the doctor achieved.

Patient	Treatment	Result
the lamb	by the doctor—gave an electrolyte solution	
	by Megan—	
the cat	by the doctor—	
	by Megan—	
the ferret	by the doctor—	
	by Megan—	

Now use your understanding of these examples to explain what the conclusion means in your own words. Write a statement that compares Megan's natural treatment to the doctor's scientific treatment.

"The elemental bonds of nature are as powerful as anything the scientific establishment has to offer" means that _____

_____

_____

_____

SELF-DEFENSE

Prereading: Biography Survey

Directions: Choose the answer that is closest to your own opinion about reading biographies and autobiographies.

1. I think reading about someone else's life is

    Ⓐ interesting because biographies are true.

    Ⓑ a way to find out what it's like to be that other person.

    Ⓒ one of my least favorite types of reading.

    Ⓓ a good way to find out what it's like to live in other times or places.

    Ⓔ my favorite kind of reading.

2. If I had the choice, I'd prefer to read about someone who

    Ⓐ is an athlete.

    Ⓑ achieved something great or heroic.

    Ⓒ writes about his or her own life.

    Ⓓ is like me.

    Ⓔ lives in a different time or place.

3. People who write biographies should

    Ⓐ stick to the facts.

    Ⓑ help readers get to know the person they're writing about inside and out.

    Ⓒ make things interesting by writing about what this person might have thought or said.

    Ⓓ write about the only life they can really know—their own.

    Ⓔ make their work as much like a novel as possible.

4. When I read about someone's life, I

    Ⓐ compare myself to the person I'm reading about.

    Ⓑ think about whether I'd like to meet this person.

    Ⓒ am inspired by what this person dreamed or accomplished.

    Ⓓ learn from that person's experience.

    Ⓔ appreciate my own life more.

SELF-DEFENSE

from *Stories from My Life*
by Cassandra Walker

Reason to read: The author thought karate class was terrifying—until she met three bullies on the street.
As you read: Think about why the author chose this title.

After baseball season ended, my parents decided it was important for my brother, Clint, and I to have an activity that we could do together a few hours a week. In other words, we were getting on our parents' nerves and they needed some time away from us.

My mom soon found what she said was the perfect activity—karate. "What? They must be joking," I thought. I told myself that there was no way I was going to hop around on some mat in bare feet, kicking sweaty people and screaming, "Ha Ya!" It was bad enough having to watch karate movies with my brother, let alone actually be in a karate class with him. Besides, I was worried I might hurt myself, or worse, break a fingernail! "That settles it," I thought, "Forget karate. How about something more civilized, like ballet?"

About a week later, we were in the car on the way to karate class, and I was pouting. My mother told me that it was important for me to learn some form of self-defense. She said I only had to stay in the class until I earned my yellow belt, which would take about two months. My brother, on the other hand, was as excited as he could be. After all, he loved karate, and this class would give him a good excuse to kick me. As I stared out the windshield, I convinced myself I wouldn't like the class at all.

We entered the class, and I noticed all sorts of trophies and awards that the instructors had earned. The room was musty and warm, and it smelled like sweaty feet. We had to take off our shoes, and we were given uniforms to change into.

There was only one other girl in the class. I was so glad to have a soul mate—someone who'd understand me, someone else who wouldn't like the idea of jumping around in white pajamas, getting kicked and chopped. In the dressing room, I introduced myself to her and said, "I don't really want to be here, how about you?" Her reply was surprising to me: "I've been trying to get my parents to let me join this class for two years. I can't wait to get out there and get going!" So much for soul mates.

In our first class, we went over the rules and

tried some karate stances. Then we were told to line up against the wall. The instructor said that it was very important for a student of karate to have a good mind and a strong body, and that at the end of every class we would be punched in the stomach to help strengthen our muscles.

"Excuse me, did he say *punched* in the stomach?!" I said to my brother.

"Yes," he replied, grinning broadly.

At that moment, I knew I had to get out of there, but it was too late. The punching had already started. All I could hear was, "Ooh, eek, ugh," then my own yell of, "OUCH!"

My parents didn't even flinch when I told them what had happened in class. "I'm sure they won't do anything to really hurt you," my father said.

"Yeah, sure they won't," I thought. "*He* doesn't have to get knocked around like a punching bag, so what does he care?"

Despite my whining, we kept going to karate class two days a week for two hours a day. After a while, I started getting the hang of it. I still didn't like the class, though, and I couldn't wait until I could quit.

One evening, my mom told us that she had an appointment and that she would be a little late picking us up from our next karate class. She gave us some money to get something at the hot dog stand after class, and she instructed us to wait for her there.

After class, Clint and I were standing at the corner waiting to cross the street and go to the hot dog stand. I noticed three teenage boys with long, stringy hair heading our way. Something told me they were up to no good. I told my brother, and he started to stuff his money in his pocket. I realized it was too late for that because the teenage boys would see what I was doing. So, I just kept my money clenched in my fist.

The boys caught up with us before the light

changed. "Give us your money or else," they said to my brother. Clint had a strange look on his face. He reluctantly handed over his money. Then the boys ran away, laughing.

My brother and I ran across the street. Clint had tears in his eyes, and I knew it was because he felt helpless. After all, those boys were a lot bigger than we were, and they outnumbered us. When our mother came to pick us up and heard what had happened, she was furious. She drove around for about an hour looking for the teenage boys, but we never found them.

Later that night, when we were getting ready for bed, my brother told me: "Even though we now know karate, there was nothing I could do about those boys. I thought that if I knew karate, I could beat anyone. Now I feel like I can't even protect myself."

I could tell he felt bad; he was used to always being the strong and protective one. Then I remembered something we had learned in karate. I said to Clint: "Remember our instructor said that part of karate is knowing when *not* to fight. You knew you were outnumbered, and if you had resisted giving the money to those boys, you could have gotten hurt and I could have, too. You were the winner today. Those boys may have been older, but you were the one who was more mature." I couldn't believe I said that to him. And I really couldn't believe that I had learned a valuable lesson in the karate class I was so determined to hate.

What I realized that day was: Every experience, no matter how new or strange or scary, can really teach you something. I had been learning things in karate class, despite my complaints. After the incident with the teenage boys, both my brother and I recognized that sometimes the best form of self-defense is to walk away from a dangerous situation.

Up Close and Personal

When you read an autobiography, you're not just reading about something that happened. You're hearing the story of the author's life in the author's own words.

How can you make the most of this chance to meet the author? Look for clues to the author's personality. The chart below will help you identify clues to Cassandra Walker's personality.

Directions: Answer the first five questions in this chart by writing phrases or sentences from the story. Answer the last two from your own experience.

Who is Cassandra Walker?

1. Is she athletic?	
2. What's her sense of humor like?	
3. How does she get along with her brother?	
4. How does she react to danger?	
5. How does she feel about learning from experience?	
6. Explain whether the author sounds like someone you'd like to have as a friend.	
7. List two ways in which you are like (or unlike) the author.	

Identifying the Author's Purpose

Columnist Cassandra Walker often writes about growing up in Chicago. She says, "I've told my story in the hopes that I might help children and teens who are feeling the self-doubt I often felt while growing up." Each chapter in Walker's *Stories from My Life* ends with her thoughts about what she learned.

Directions: Answer the questions below to find out why the author chose to tell this story.

1. **Situation:** Describe the confrontation and why Cassandra decides not to fight.

   _____

   _____

   _____

2. **Lesson:** Summarize the advice Cassandra gives her brother about handling a dangerous situation.

   _____

   _____

   _____

3. **Conclusion:** Find a sentence in the story that explains the meaning of the title.

   _____

   _____

   _____

4. **Your opinion:** Explain whether you agree or disagree with the author's conclusion. Give at least two reasons for your answer.

   _____

   _____

   _____

BRANCH RICKEY SIGNS JACKIE ROBINSON

Prereading: Baseball's Color Barrier

Directions: The left column describes how black Americans were treated when baseball's "color barrier" was enforced. Complete the chart by contrasting conditions in 1945 to conditions today.

In 1945	Today
Many restaurants and hotels refused to serve African Americans.	
African American baseball players could only play on all-black teams. They had their own league, called the "Negro League."	
Some ball parks made black fans sit in a segregated, or separate, section.	
Many white fans did not believe that black athletes could perform well in the major leagues.	

Use this information to explain below your ideas about what the term *color barrier* means.

_____

_____

_____

BRANCH RICKEY SIGNS JACKIE ROBINSON

from *Jackie Robinson and the Breaking of the Color Barrier*
by Russell Shorto

Reason to read: Find out why this contract offer made baseball history.
As you read: Think about what it would be like to meet the challenges Jackie Robinson faced.

"Mr. Baseball"—that was one of Branch Rickey's nicknames. He was one of the most important people in the history of the game. He invented the farm club system, which allowed young players to gain experience playing organized baseball in the minor leagues.

But Branch Rickey's biggest contribution was to help Jackie Robinson break the color barrier. This had been a dream of Rickey's for many years. In 1910, he was the coach of a college team in Ohio. One day, the team traveled to South Bend, Indiana, for a game. The whites on the team checked into a hotel, but the manager of the hotel would not let the team's one black player check in. He said the hotel did not accept blacks. Finally, Branch Rickey got the manager to let the player stay with Rickey on a cot in his room. Later that night, the player sat up crying because he felt so ashamed and hurt. Branch Rickey never forgot that painful scene.

He got his chance to change things in 1945, when he signed Jackie Robinson. Many old-timers were furious. Once, after he gave a speech about integration, a man came up to him and tried to wrestle him to the ground. But these incidents soon stopped. Over the next few years, every pro team signed black players. An important step in the civil rights movement had been taken.

[When Rickey offered Jackie a contract, he wanted to be sure that Jackie understood the pressure he'd face. "We can't fight our way through this, Jackie," he said. "We can win only if we can convince the world that I'm doing this because you're a great ballplayer and a fine gentleman." Then Rickey went on to call Jackie some of the names he'd be called by fans and other ball-players.]

"Can you take that?" Rickey asked. He wanted Jackie to understand that as the first black player in the major leagues, he would get a lot of racial abuse. He wanted to make sure Jackie would "turn the other cheek" and ignore the abuse, rather than try to fight back. If Jackie argued, he could ruin the chances of other black players who might follow him. It would be better to show America that he was above name-calling. He had to impress the nation with his baseball skills, not his fighting skills.

Jackie was not sure he liked this. He asked if Rickey was looking for a black player who was afraid to fight back.

Branch Rickey's eyes lit up. "I'm looking for a ballplayer with guts enough *not* to fight back!" he cried. "Can you do it?"

Jackie thought for a while. Then he said, "I think I can."

"Thinking isn't enough," Rickey told him. "Can you?"

Jackie made up his mind. He had learned a lot

from his mother. One of her lessons was that it is often wiser to turn the other cheek than to fight back. "I can," Jackie said.

That year, Jackie and [his girlfriend] Rachel [Isum] were finally married. Soon afterward, Jackie appeared at the training camp of the Montreal Royals, one of the Dodgers' farm clubs. A farm club is a team in the minor leagues in which promising players show whether or not they have enough talent to play in the majors.

Jackie would have to prove himself in Montreal. Some fans there were angry, but others were curious to see how well a black would play in the minors. They soon got their answer.

The first game of the Royals' 1946 season was played in Jersey City, New Jersey. The stadium was packed with a sellout crowd of 52,000. People were happy because World War II was over and because the start of a new baseball season is always a time of celebration. Everyone was also eager to see the league's first black player. As the national anthem played, Jackie Robinson felt a lump in his throat and a nervous quiver in his stomach. He knew everyone was there to see him.

Jackie was the second batter. The first batter grounded out. Then Jackie walked to the plate in a funny pigeon-toed way that would soon become famous. He was stocky and thickly muscled. He watched a fastball zip past and did not swing. Then a second flew across the plate. Finally, on the third pitch, he swung the bat. The ball bounced to the shortstop, who threw to first base. Jackie Robinson was out.

People in the stands looked at one another. They had heard that Robinson was a great hitter. But it did not take a great hitter to ground out. Some wondered whether he would make it to the big leagues.

Jackie came up to bat again in the third inning. Now there were two men on base and no outs. The other team had heard that Jackie was a great

bunter. They thought he would try to bunt, so the infield moved in close. The pitcher wound up and threw a hard fastball.

Crack! The ball sailed in a high arc over the left field fence. Jackie Robinson had hit a home run! Three runs were scored on the hit, and the crowd erupted into cheers. Jackie got three more hits in the game and stole two bases. The Royals went on to win, 14 to 1. Newspapers reported that Jackie Robinson had stolen the show and had proved that blacks deserved a place in major league baseball.

It was a great year. Jackie Robinson led his team to the International League championship and finished his first season as the league's batting champ. He also led the league in runs scored.

Black America was proud. A few years earlier, Joe Louis, the boxing champ, had been the hero of young blacks around the nation. Now they also cheered on Jackie Robinson, the hero of the minor leagues.

[Jackie's success earned him a contract with the Brooklyn Dodgers. During his first two years in the majors, he recalled, "I was an exhibit in a glass cage—a tiger who had been trained not to roar. The day would come when I could roar as loudly as I wished and whenever I pleased. Maybe during these days when I couldn't fight back I could help to fix it so there would be less to roar about in days to come."

During Jackie's first season, his teammates began defending him when the fans yelled insults or opposing players spiked him. Then *Sporting News*, which had predicted he'd fail, named him Rookie of the Year. Jackie played nine more seasons in the major leagues. His team, the Brooklyn Dodgers, won six National League Pennants and the 1955 World Series. In 1956, he won the Springarn medal. He was elected to the National Baseball Hall of Fame in 1962.]

A Question of Character

Jackie Robinson was not the only talented black player of his time. What convinced Rickey that this athlete was the best person to break the color barrier? Russell Shorto answers this question by showing how Jackie Robinson responded to several challenges. Usually the author describes Robinson's actions. He includes other responses as well, such as Robinson's thoughts.

Directions: Complete the chart by giving examples of how Robinson responded to each challenge. Rereading parts of the selection may be helpful.

Challenge	Robinson's Response(s)
"I'm looking for a ballplayer with guts enough not to fight back!" [Branch Rickey] cried. "Can you do it?"	Robinson's thoughts
	Robinson's beliefs
	Robinson's words
Fans wondered if a black athlete could play well in the minor leagues.	Robinson's actions
Branch Rickey warned, "We can win only if we can convince the world that I'm doing this because you're a great ballplayer and a fine gentleman."	Robinson's actions
	People's reaction to Robinson

Cause and Effect

In this selection, the author describes how Branch Rickey and Jackie Robinson broke baseball's color barrier. The chart below shows three important changes that they accomplished.

Directions: Use information from the selection to complete the chart. Complete the second column by identifying what made the change happen. In the third column, explain what happened as a result of the change.

Before the Change	Cause of Change	Effect of Change
1. A black player on Rickey's college team was shamed when he was denied a hotel room.	Rickey was moved by the player's distress. He dreamed that one day black players would be able to play on any professional baseball team.	
2. Many people did not believe black ballplayers belonged in the major leagues.	Jackie Robinson was the best hitter and base stealer in his league.	
3. Rickey knew that the first black to play in the major leagues had to ignore racial abuse instead of fighting back.		Soon every professional baseball team had at least one black player.

ALL IN A DAY'S WORK

Prereading: The Perfect Job

Biographies often include information about a person's whole life. But authors don't always cover their subject from birth to death. Sometimes they describe just one typical day.

This selection is about one day in the life of a television reporter. Before you read it, think about the kind of work you'd like to do after you finish school.

Directions: Describe a typical day (or night) on your ideal job.

Job: _____

9:00 a.m./p.m.

11:00 a.m./p.m.

1:00 a.m./p.m.

3:00 a.m./p.m.

5:00 a.m./p.m.

ALL IN A DAY'S WORK

from *All in a Day's Work: Twelve Americans Talk About Their Jobs*
by Neil Johnson

Reason to read: Reading about a reporter at work is one way to find out if you'd like that job.
As you read: Identify what Christie Walton likes and dislikes about her job.

Christie Walton was a television reporter for several years, specializing in feature stories rather than hard news. She still does some reporting on weekdays, but the main part of her job now involves **anchoring** (presenting most of the news on camera), **producing** (writing the news and deciding what goes where), and being assignment editor (deciding what stories need to be covered) for the Saturday and Sunday newscasts.

The term *journalist* refers loosely to the act of going out, finding out about something, and then communicating that information to someone else. Involved in that are an awful lot of decisions: Is it important? Why is it important? Why should the viewer care? We want to do the essence of the story,

A journalist interviews a foreign dignitary.

the "Who? What? Where? When? Why?," but we also need to consider the viewers. How does this story affect their lives? *Does* it affect their lives? Why should Joe Six-Pack, John Doe out there, care about the story? That has a lot to do with whether we'll cover a story.

Some people would call what I do for a living "being nosy" or "digging in somebody else's business" or being a kind of vulture. And in a strange sense, that may be true. We're waiting for some-

thing to go wrong so we can make a story out of it. But at the same time, if we are uncovering or doing a story about a public official who is stealing money, there is a public interest in that, because it's not just that official who's affected. It's all of the people who pay the taxes.

But there are parts of this job that don't suit my personality—the part where I have to make people angry. People sometimes have to be asked "the hard question," the question I know they aren't going to want to hear. And they aren't going to like me because I've asked it. Very often I will go into a situation that is not pleasant, and that is one of the reasons that I don't do very much hard news. I prefer to do feature stories. But in some instances, the importance of that hard question overrides my desire to be liked. In the instance of a recent story on allegations of child abuse, my interest in that—the belief that maybe there is a wrong here—made it easier for me to ask tough questions. I hoped the person that I asked respected the fact that I was only doing my job.

One of the best things about this job is that when I walk in the door each day I don't know what I'm going to be doing. It's something different every day. Some days I may sit at my desk and make phone calls and get information and never leave the building. I like anchoring an awful lot, but I think my favorite part of the job is meeting the people—going out and never knowing who I'm going to meet. I meet regular people on the street who tell me their opinion of something on the news. I've met rock stars like Brian Adams. I've had a chance to meet senators and develop friendships with congressmen, because I cover them a lot. I've met a whole spectrum of people. I've met people who are so off the wall you wouldn't believe it, and people who are so incredibly intelligent that they make you feel like the most ignorant slime in the world!

My least favorite part of the job is the deadlines. The time! The highest pressure is making that deadline. It's getting the best information I can, the best picture I can, getting them laid down and edited in time. The pressure is frustrating, but it's a piece of the job. I work within the time constraints, because no one is going to say, "Oh, we'll put off the six o'clock news and wait for your story to be finished." I learned that when I need to work quickly, I work quickly. And I do the work without ignoring facts or details and without losing those basic premises that we work on: the "Who? What? When? Where? and Why?" And I try to show it in a compelling way.

I may do an hour interview and still not think I've gotten what I needed. I may have to pull fifteen, twenty seconds out of that. So I make choices. I'm a **gatekeeper** for this information in a lot of ways. I decide what to let the interviewed subject say and what I can say. I choose what we call "sound bites"—snippets of a conversation from an interview—to impart some information. I hope that ten or fifteen seconds says something. Amazing enough, a lot can be said in that amount of time.

I suppose my job is like any other. Not every

day is going to be the big story—there is a lot of boredom that goes along with the job. But some days, it's exciting to get to work because I know I'll be working on something that I've really gotten excited about, something I really want to tell people about. The best news stories are the ones that are told in the way that you would walk up to a friend and say, "Can you believe what happened today? You should see!" That's the excitement of this business, because it has become the "back fence" of our society. It's the talking. It's a personal form of communication, and that's exciting to me—that intimacy that television brings.

When I'm on the air, I'm in people's bedrooms, in their kitchens, in their cars—I'm in a lot of aspects of people's lives! Very intimate! That's scary at times, because people know me and know a lot about me, and I've never seen them. And they feel a connection with me, personally. They feel like they own a little piece of me sometimes. I have lost an aspect of anonymity. What I do is very much under scrutiny by the people around me. I will go to the grocery store in my oldest sweat suit and tennis shoes, and someone will see me and go, "Well, golly! You don't look like that on TV!" I'm used to it and I laugh with them. I say, "Yeah, the makeup does a great job, doesn't it!"

Job Jargon

Does Christie Walton know how to be a good television reporter? You can answer that question even if you've never seen her on camera. She sets high standards for her work. And she uses several words that show she knows her job. For example, she talks about *sound bites*, or short quotations selected from a taped interview.

Words used by people with expert knowledge of a job are called *jargon*. This expert language can be confusing to those who don't do the same work. But jargon allows experts to communicate quickly and precisely among themselves. This activity will help you determine the meaning of the jargon terms used by the reporter.

Directions: Each of the words below has several dictionary meanings. Two meanings are given. Write your own definition of what Christie Walton means when she uses the word. If you need help, find the **bold** word in the selection and reread the sentences around it.

1. **anchoring**

   dropping a weight into the water to hold a ship in place
   running the last leg of a relay race

   _____

2. **producing**

   raising food
   manufacturing

   _____

3. **journalist**

   someone who keeps a journal or diary
   writer who tries to reach a large audience

   _____

4. **gatekeeper**

   someone who guards a gate
   someone who controls access

   _____

The Five W's

Christie Walton lists five questions that cover the most important parts of any news story: Who? What? Where? When? Why? Reporters call these "the five W's." Good reporters don't stop there. They go on to ask "How?"

After reporters ask these questions, they arrange the answers from most important to least important. A story about the results of the presidential election would probably begin with *who* won. A news item about an earthquake would feature *where* it happened.

Directions: The chart below will help you find the most important ideas in the article about Christie Walton. Use information from the story to answer the questions below.

W's and H	Answers
Who is Christie Walton?	
Why does she think her job is important?	
Why does she prefer doing human interest stories to doing hard news?	
What does she like best about her job?	
What does she like least about her job?	
When is she most excited about her work?	
How does she feel about being recognized by so many people?	
Where do you think she finds the greatest satisfaction in her work? Give an example from the selection to support your answer.	

SINKING STOMACHS AND FLOATING MOVIE STARS

by Wim Coleman and Pat Perrin

Reason to read: Learn about g-forces.
As you read: Think of headings that could go in the numbered boxes.

What causes that giddy feeling when you're on a roller coaster starting down a steep slope? Or those rocks in your belly when it reaches the bottom? What pushes the driver back into his seat when a jet-powered car really takes off? And why is a certain jet plane nicknamed the "Vomit Comet"?

The answers to these questions have to do with g-forces. Whether you know it or not, you're feeling g-forces right now. If you weren't, you'd float away into the air! The letter g stands for gravity. If you're sitting or standing without moving, you are feeling one g. This is the normal pull of gravity.

1.

Sometimes, the number of g's pulling at our bodies changes. Suppose you get on an elevator and push the button to go up. Suddenly, the elevator starts to move, and you feel heavy. This increase in speed is called acceleration. And in this case, it increases the g-forces pulling you downward. It causes you to feel more than one g.

Soon, the elevator quits accelerating and moves at a constant speed. You feel normal again because you're back to just one g. At last, the elevator begins to slow. For a moment, you feel light. This decrease in speed is called deceleration. And in this case, it decreases the g-forces pulling you downward. It causes you to feel less than one g.

Acceleration and deceleration can work the other way around. For example, suppose you get on an elevator and push a button to take you down. The elevator accelerates, but instead of feeling heavy, you feel light. Then, when the elevator decelerates, you feel heavy.

A roller coaster changes g-forces too, but in a much more dramatic way. Imagine you're in a roller coaster at the top of a rise, suddenly accelerating downward. At that moment, you feel as light as a butterfly! Then, at the bottom of the slope, the track abruptly levels out. At that moment, you feel like you've got rocks in your stomach! The g's you feel in a roller coaster are much greater than those of an elevator. The Moonslaut Scramble in Japan produces g's as high as 6.5.

Even in your family car, you can feel a change in g-forces. These usually push you backwards or forwards instead of up or down. When an ordinary car accelerates, it pushes you back into your seat with a force of about 1.2 g's. When the car reaches a steady speed, you're back to one g again. If the car suddenly decelerates, g-forces will drop, and you'll feel like you're being pulled forward in your seat.

2.

Racing cars cause greater changes in g-forces. For example, a kind of racing car called a funny car is powered by a jet engine. This engine is equipped with what's called an afterburner. The afterburner sprays fresh fuel into the exhaust. The mixture of gas and air ignites the fuel, doubling the engine's thrust. (Some military aircraft also use afterburners. They can be helpful for a quick take-off or an escape.)

When the afterburner kicks in, the car speeds up. Then the driver might feel a 4.8 g-force. To stop the car, a parachute opens and the engine shuts off. Then the driver might suddenly feel 7 times lighter than normal. This condition is called negative g's.

3.

G-forces play an important role in space travel. Astronauts experience great changes in g's. This is a big part of what makes space travel so dangerous. Space travel involves getting a spacecraft into orbit, which means circling the earth at very high altitudes. Escaping the earth's gravity requires tremendous acceleration. Between liftoff and orbit, astronauts undergo between 3 and 6 g's.

Coming out of orbit also creates high g-forces. An unmanned satellite decelerating from orbit can undergo 60 g's! No human being could survive that pressure. But in the days of manned space capsules, astronauts endured as many as 10 g's coming out of orbit. The space shuttle has changed this. Its wings allow it to decelerate

more slowly. So in a shuttle, astronauts only experience 1.5 g's when coming out of orbit. This isn't much greater than the acceleration of a family car.

The g's endured by astronauts may not sound like much. After all, a Japanese roller coaster produces 6.5 g's. But there's an important difference. On roller coasters or in funny cars, g's rise for only seconds at a time. Getting into orbit can take nine minutes! That's a long time to weigh much more than usual. What's more, prolonged g's can be dangerous. At five g's, an astronaut's blood weighs the same as iron. If g's go up from there, the lungs begin to fill with blood. Breathing gets very difficult. Astronauts must be in excellent condition to withstand such pressure.

While in orbit, astronauts experience something even stranger than high g's. They feel like they weigh nothing at all! Physicists call this microgravity. The spacecraft is still under the influence of the earth's gravity. But the astronauts can't feel it. So astronauts call this condition zero g's or zero gravity.

4.

In zero g's, astronauts float about the cabin if they're not strapped in. So will anything which isn't locked down. What does zero gravity feel like? A Hollywood movie team found out.

In 1995, film director Ron Howard released a movie called *Apollo 13*. It was about an almost-fatal 1970 space flight. Howard wanted to show audiences what weightlessness was like. So he rented a jet called the KC-135. It is owned by NASA, the National Aeronautics and Space Administration. The KC-135 is used to train astronauts for weightlessness.

The plane begins by climbing to 36,000 feet. Then it suddenly dives. It keeps on diving for 23 seconds. While it's diving, everybody aboard feels

weightless! The pilots, of course, are strapped into their seats. But astronaut trainees are put in a padded chamber. They float freely inside while the plane dives. For 23 seconds, they feel no g-forces at all.

In the movie *Apollo 13*, the astronauts were played by actors Tom Hanks, Bill Paxton, and Kevin Bacon. All three of them were trained aboard the KC-135. Then a movie set was built inside the plane to represent the cabin of the Apollo 13. Several scenes were filmed in actual weightlessness.

Everybody had trouble adjusting to zero gravity. Astronaut trainees often get sick when they experience it for the first time. This is why the KC-135 is nicknamed the "Vomit Comet." The movie stars and crews had trouble too. On one flight, a cam-

eraman threw up all over Kevin Bacon.

Of course, astronauts in orbit are weightless for much longer than 23 seconds. Some have spent many months in zero g's. Even so, scientists aren't sure about the long-term effects of weightlessness. Perhaps astronauts can adapt to zero g's indefinitely. But then they may find it hard to get used to the earth's gravity again.

We humans seem to enjoy playing with our g levels. We even find it fun. If we didn't, we wouldn't ride roller coasters. But we should feel grateful that our bodies and the earth's gravity make such a good fit. Our blood circulation, muscle tone, and sense of balance work best in one g because that's what we grew up in. Small wonder we feel more at home with our feet on the ground!

Writing Subheads

Articles in science textbooks and magazines are often broken into smaller units. Each unit, or section, is titled with a *subhead.* These subheads tell the reader what to expect in each section of the article.

Directions: In the the article "Sinking Stomachs and Floating Movie Stars," there are four empty boxes where subheads could go. For the first three subheads, select the answer that you believe best summarizes the section that follows. Come up with your own subhead for the last section.

1. Subhead #1

   Ⓐ g-forces in elevators

   Ⓑ g-forces in our everyday lives

   Ⓒ acceleration

   Ⓓ acceleration and deceleration

2. Subhead #2

   Ⓐ afterburners

   Ⓑ deceleration

   Ⓒ acceleration

   Ⓓ g-forces in funny cars

3. Subhead #3

   Ⓐ g-forces in space travel

   Ⓑ how astronauts get in shape for travel

   Ⓒ zero g and its effects

   Ⓓ acceleration and deceleration

4. Subhead #4

   _____

Charting G-Forces

A picture is worth a thousand words. This familiar saying is really true when it comes to charts and graphs. *Charts* and *graphs* convert numbers into pictures. So they make it easy to see number relationships at a glance.

Directions: The bar graph below shows the g-forces of eight situations mentioned in the article. All but one label is blank. Refer to the article to complete the labels. For example, the article says that "when an ordinary car accelerates, it pushes you back into your seat with a force of about 1.2 g's." Note that the line on the x axis by the 1.2 g bar is labeled "Family car acceleration."

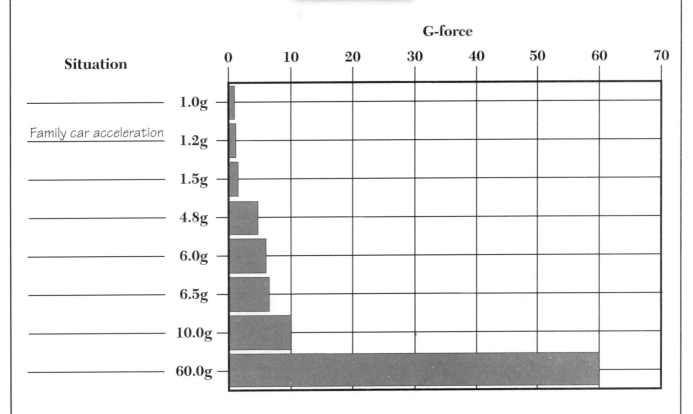

Situations

Family car acceleration   Roller coaster
Funny car acceleration   Unmanned probe deceleration
Normal Earth gravity   Acceleration to achieve orbit
Space shuttle reentry   Space capsule reentry

A Glossary of Technical Terms

When experts write articles, they often use technical terms that are specific to the topic. For example, a computer specialist may write about her P100 with 32 MB of RAM and a 1.2 gig hard drive. In plainer language, the specialist is describing the amount of memory and storage space in her computer.

Directions: In the activity below, you are going to prepare a glossary of terms for "Sinking Stomachs and Floating Movie Stars." First, find the terms listed below in the article. Write short definitions for each term. Add other technical terms from the article to complete the glossary.

Hint: The authors usually include a definition when they first use a term.

acceleration: _____

afterburner: _____

astronaut: _____

deceleration: _____

funny car: _____

g-force: _____

KC-135: _____

microgravity: _____

NASA: _____

_____ _____

_____ _____

_____ _____

_____ _____

_____ _____

_____ _____

_____ _____

Prereading: Weighing the Evidence

Suppose the first thing you hear when you get to school is, "I saw a giant purple elephant last night!" Would you believe or doubt this statement?

People who have never seen a giant purple elephant might doubt the statement. But strange things do happen. How do you decide whether this claim is true or not? The activity below suggests some ways you can weigh the evidence for and against the statement.

Directions: Place a **+** in the blank by any piece of evidence that would make you believe someone who said, "I saw a giant purple elephant." Put a **-** in the blank by any piece of evidence that would make you doubt this statement.

Who said it?

_____ someone who's always playing practical jokes

_____ someone whose honesty is well-known

Who else saw it?

_____ the practical joker's best friend

_____ an officer in the National Guard

What physical evidence is there?

_____ a large footprint three inches deep

_____ a photograph of a large purple elephant floating in mid-air

Is there any other explanation for the physical evidence?

_____ You see a large foot attached to a stick fall out of the jokester's locker.

_____ The photograph has a caption describing a float in the Parade of Fantastic Creatures.

THE LIZARD IN THE LOCH

by Cynthia M. Martin

Reason to read: Think about evidence for and against the existence of a strange creature.
As you read: Decide whether you believe or disbelieve in this creature.

Question: What has no legs, two legs, *or* four legs; has black, gray, brown, *or* green skin; has no horns, two horns, *or* three horns; and has one, two, three, *or* six humps? Answer: The Loch Ness Monster, known as Nessie to her friends. This giant sea serpent may or may not live in Loch Ness, a deep lake in Scotland.

Loch Ness is one of the strangest lakes in the world. It is 24 miles long, but only one mile wide. The lake is more than 700 feet deep in spots. In addition, the water is full of peat, a kind of soil. This makes the water so murky that divers can't see more than a foot or two in front of them.

But the strangest thing about Loch Ness is the monster that may live in the water. Some people believe in the monster. Others think it is a giant hoax. There's evidence to support both sides of the question.

This photo, taken by Dr. Kenneth Wilson in 1934, was considered the best evidence that Nessie exists. However, on his deathbed, Wilson admitted that he faked the photo.
AP/Wide World Photos

Why Nessie May Be Real

First, many people have said that they have seen the monster. The first recorded report took place in 565 A.D. An Irish missionary known as St. Columba spotted "an odd-looking beastie" that was about to eat a local resident. The saint told the creature to "go back at once!", and the monster disappeared under the waves.

Since then, more than 3,000 people have reported Nessie sightings. Their descriptions vary. Some people see humps in the water. Some see a large gray eye peering at them. One student saw Nessie cross the road in front of his bicycle. Alexander Campbell, a conservationist who lives near the lake, has seen the creature 18 times. Even Richard Synge, a Nobel prize-winning chemist, admitted that he once saw the creature in the loch.

Second, there is scientific evidence. People have taken pictures of the creature. They have spotted tracks along the shore. One man even shot home movies of Nessie. In 1987, a group of scientists came to Loch Ness. They brought a boat equipped with sonar, a type of underwater tracking device. They tracked a moving object that was more than 20 feet long. Was this Nessie?

Finally, Nessie may have cousins. People have reported seeing strange creatures in several other lakes in the world. New York's Lake Champlain has Champ, a beast who looks a lot like Nessie. Canada's Lake Okanagan has Nitaka, the "snake of the water." Some local Native Americans believed in this creature and used to sacrifice a chicken to it whenever they crossed the lake. None of the people living on these lakes knew each other; they lived hundreds of miles apart. Yet they all reported seeing similar creatures. Could they all be wrong?

Why Nessie May Be Fake

Since 1933, hundreds of people have looked for the Loch Ness Monster. Scientists have used boats and submarines to explore the lake. Fishermen have tried capturing the creature in nets or spearing it with harpoons. One man even built a 25-foot steel cage. People have spent weeks sitting next to the lake with a camera, hoping to get just one good shot. However, no one has ever captured Nessie. No body has ever washed up on shore. No one has found any strange bones. No one has discovered any Nessie eggs. Despite all the searches, there is no solid proof that Nessie exists.

Yes, many people have spotted something in the lake. But people often see what they want to see. Someone who has driven hundreds of miles to look for a monster may see a tree stump and think, "There's Nessie!"

What about the photographs? The most famous picture was taken in 1934 by a man named Kenneth Wilson. Just before his death, he admitted that the creature in his famous photo was a rubber model! There are other photos of Nessie, but they are blurred and unclear. Some show only a hump, or a bump that could be a tree branch. Some photos show the water

rippling on the surface of the lake. Almost anything can cause ripples on the water. And no one has a clear picture of a whole creature. Even the sonar images don't tell us for sure that there is a creature in that lake.

Finally, there is another explanation for Nessie. The legend brings thousands of people to Loch Ness each year. The visitors stay in local motels. They buy gas for their cars and film for their cameras. They eat at local restaurants. They buy Nessie paperweights and t-shirts. The whole story of Nessie may be nothing more than a clever tourist attraction. One local innkeeper even claims that his father "created" Nessie in 1934, after reading a book of old stories.

The legend lives on. People are still looking for the Loch Ness Monster today. We may never know what Nessie is, or even if she exists. However, if you're ever in Scotland, perhaps you might like to visit Loch Ness. Who knows? Maybe Nessie will decide to come out and play.

Residents of the Loch Ness area search for signs of Nessie.
UPI/Corbis-Bettmann

THE LIZARD IN THE LOCH

Using Context Clues

Skilled readers can often find the meaning of unfamiliar words by studying the way these words are used. This is called *using context clues*. Among the types of context clues are

- **definition.** The writer uses a word and then gives its meaning or uses a synonym.
- **comparison/contrast.** The word is contrasted to a word with the opposite meaning.
- **examples.** Details or examples show the word's meaning.

Directions: Complete the chart below by writing a definition of each **bold** word in the second column. Then in the last column identify the type of context clue you used.

Word in Context	Definition	Type of Context Clue
1. "…the water is full of **peat,** a kind of soil."	*peat* means:	Ⓐ definition Ⓑ comparison/contrast Ⓒ example
2. "This [soil] makes the water so **murky** that divers can't see more than a foot or two in front of them."	*murky* means:	Ⓐ definition Ⓑ comparison/contrast Ⓒ example
3. "Some people believe in the monster. Others think it is a giant **hoax."**	a *hoax* is:	Ⓐ definition Ⓑ comparison/contrast Ⓒ example
4. "They brought a boat equipped with **sonar,** a type of underwater tracking device."	*sonar* is:	Ⓐ definition Ⓑ comparison/contrast Ⓒ example
5. "Fishermen have tried capturing the creature in nets or spearing it with a **harpoon."**	a *harpoon* is:	Ⓐ definition Ⓑ comparison/contrast Ⓒ example

Fact or Hoax?

This article presents both sides of a controversial issue: Does the Loch Ness monster exist? Many people believe that there is evidence, or proof, that Nessie is real. However, doubters have questions about each piece of evidence. How do you answer a question like this?

Directions: One way to resolve a controversy is to review all of the evidence. Read the evidence in the first column below. Then decide whether you accept or reject that evidence. Use the second column. Finally, review the amount of evidence you accepted. Is that enough to prove that Nessie is real? Write your answer in the box labeled Your Conclusion.

Evidence That Nessie Is Real	Reasons to Accept/Reject Evidence
1. Many people have seen a large, serpent-like creature. They include reputable people such as a saint and a Nobel prize-winner.	This evidence Ⓐ proves Ⓑ does not prove that Nessie exists because…
2. Scientific evidence includes photos, tracks, home movies, and sonar tracings.	This evidence Ⓐ proves Ⓑ does not prove that Nessie exists because…
3. Similar creatures have been sighted around the world.	This evidence Ⓐ proves Ⓑ does not prove that Nessie exists because…
4. The best explanation of all of this evidence is that a giant serpent-like creature lives in Loch Ness.	The best explanation is that…

Your Conclusion

TALL CITY OF SILENT STONE

from *Lost Cities*
by Joyce Goldenstern

Reason to read: Learn about the adventures of the scientist who discovered a lost city.
As you read: Notice how archaeologists interpret clues from the past.

"It fairly took my breath away. What could this place be? Why had no one given us any idea of it?" With these words, Hiram Bingham remembered his first view of Machu Picchu, in 1911. For centuries the ancient city had been deserted. Hidden in a remote area of Peru, it had not attracted visitors. Bingham felt the city's loneliness and majesty. His journey there had been a trying one, but the splendor before his eyes made it worth the effort.

High in the Andes

The Inca had ruled in the Andes Mountains from about A.D. 1430 to A.D. 1532. Hiram Bingham had come to Peru hoping to find Inca ceremonial sites. A local farmer had encouraged Bingham to seek ruins on a mountain ridge called Machu Picchu. To get there, Bingham, who was not in good physical shape, first crossed rapids of a roaring river. A rickety bridge—some logs tied together with vines—offered the only way across. Bingham wrote, "No one could live for an instant in the icy cold rapids." They would "immediately be dashed to pieces against the rocks." Bingham got down on his stomach to crawl slowly across the bridge, creeping along "six inches at a time."

Workers restore the Inca fortress of Machu Picchu.

The most dangerous part of the journey lay ahead. Soon after he crossed the river, he found himself at the bottom of a steep slope. For over an hour he climbed, clawing the dirt with his fingernails. The heat and extreme humidity seemed more than he could bear. Several times he thought he would fall to his death, but finally he lifted himself up to the top of the slope.

He came upon a small hut where two farmers lived. They were descendants of highland Indians who had lived in the Inca empire. One of the farmers brought Bingham cool water in a drinking gourd. They allowed him to rest, gave him sweet potatoes to eat, and provided him with a young guide who would show him some ruins.

The guide led him to "beautifully constructed stone-faced terraces." Bingham marveled at a curved temple and other structures. "Surprise followed surprise," he wrote. Most amazing was the stonework. With great artistic ability, the Incas had cut stones into fine geometrical shapes, each stone fitting perfectly together with another without any glue or mortar between them. Bingham could not even slip the slender blade of a knife through the stone fittings. The stones "might have grown together," Bingham wrote.

Making Sense • INFORMATION

Figuring Out the Clues

Bingham wanted to identify the ruins, but jungle growth covered many of them. Bingham wrote that "massive trees, two feet thick, perched on the gable ends of small…houses." He needed help. After a month or so, he left Machu Picchu. Within a year, he returned with workers who helped him chop away the jungle plants that hid the structures. The city that emerged amazed him. He tried to guess the use of each building; he wrote and spoke about his find. Soon other archaeologists arrived, and gradually a story about the Inca unfolded.

How can a deserted city tell a story? Think of a similar, modern example. Imagine that a family is far away from home. A stranger walks into their home and heads for a teenage boy's bedroom. The stranger wants to learn about the teenager by looking at his room. She notices that the bed is unmade. The clothes are strewn about. She looks at a CD collection and plays a few selections. She admires his aquarium and even feeds the fish. She finds some magazines and books under the bed. She writes their titles in a small notebook. She sketches the likeness of a poster she notices on the wall. She looks out the window and observes the bustling street below. Has the stranger learned anything about the teenager? Has the bedroom told a story?

A lost city cannot tell a complete story, but it can offer hints and clues, adding to a story that others have told. The Inca had no written language. Officials kept records with *quipa*, a system of counting that used knots on a cord. The knots are evidence of the Inca accounting system, but they do not tell us a lot about daily life. By looking at ruins, archaeologists can tell more about the Inca: They built roads, and they mastered stone architecture. They ruled an empire that extended north and south from Ecuador to Chile, stretching 2,500 miles. Such accomplishments require a lot of organization. Strong leaders must have exercised great power over lowly workers who carried the stones needed to build the temples and walls and roads.

When archaeologists investigated the ruins of Machu Picchu, they learned even more. They found many temples and shrines—more than had been found in most Inca cities. It seemed that Machu Picchu may have had special religious significance, as Bingham had thought. He liked to brag that Machu Picchu was the original, mythological home of Inca ancestors. Most archaeologists disagreed with him because none of the buildings showed evidence of the simple early Inca style. They thought that the Inca probably built the city in the 1500s, at the peak of their power. It was not their first home, but still it was probably a sacred place.

There are other clues today about the ancient Inca. Some of their descendants continue practicing what they say are old ways, and it is possible that some of their customs are similar to customs of the ancient Inca. For example, the descendants still live in the highland mountains, farming and weaving in a traditional manner.

Geography and climate are also helpful for understanding daily life in the past. Farming is difficult in high, rocky mountains. The stone terraces built by the Inca probably helped to level the land for farming.

It is also possible to learn about the Inca from their conquerors. The Inca were at the height of their power when the Spanish arrived in Peru in the 1500s. Some Spaniards recorded their impressions of the civilization. These writings help tell the story, but they must be read carefully, because they are not always fair or accurate. One Spanish historian of the 1500s described the Inca as "sheep without a shepherd." In general, the Spaniards saw the Inca as enemies. They wanted Inca land and treasures, so their accounts were biased.

Making Educated Guesses

Like readers, scientists sometimes have to *infer,* or make educated guesses, about the subjects they are studying. The scientific term for such guesses is *hypotheses.* For example, a scientist may hypothesize that an ancient city was an important trade center. The scientist would then look for facts, or clues, to prove or disprove the guess. The chart below will help you tell a statement of fact from an educated guess.

Hints: How can you recognize an educated guess? Look for words or phrases that signal an opinion or educated guess. The list below will help you recognize such statements.

it seems	must have	probably
perhaps	it is possible	it is likely

Directions: Study the statements in the chart below. First decide whether each one is an educated guess or a statement of fact. Then identify the clues you used to determine whether the statement is a fact or an educated guess. The first one is done for you.

Statement	Fact or Guess	Clues
1. "The Inca had cut stones into fine geometric shapes."	● fact Ⓑ educated guess	*This is a statement of fact because Bingham reported it.*
2. "The Inca had no written language. Officials kept records with a *quipa,* a system of counting that used knots on a cord."	Ⓐ fact Ⓑ educated guess	
3. "[The Inca] ruled an empire that extended north and south from Ecuador to Chile, stretching 2,500 miles."	Ⓐ fact Ⓑ educated guess	
4. "Strong leaders must have exercised great power over lowly workers who carried the stones needed to build the temples…and roads."	Ⓐ fact Ⓑ educated guess	
5. "It seemed that Machu Picchu may have had special religious significance, as Bingham had thought."	Ⓐ fact Ⓑ educated guess	
6. "The stone terraces built by the Inca probably helped to level the land for farming."	Ⓐ fact Ⓑ educated guess	

Word Parts and Word Play

Hiram Bingham was an *archaeologist*—someone who studies early human life. This word is made up of two parts: *archae-*, which means ancient or primitive; and *-ologist*, which means a person who studies a science. When you put the two parts together you get *archaeologist,* a person who studies ancient or primitive things.

Directions: Study the prefixes, roots, and suffixes in the chart below. Then answer the questions that follow.

Prefixes	Roots	Suffixes
archae—ancient, primitive **bio**—life **geo**—earth	**anthrop**—human **chem**—chemical	**ist** or **ologist**—one who studies a science **ology**—the science or study of

1. What does the word *biologist* mean?_____

2. What does the word *geology* mean? _____

3. What would a person who studies the earth be called? _____

4. What would a person who studies people be called? _____

5. What would a person who studies chemicals be called? _____

6. What would the study of life be called? _____

Your Turn

Use the word parts below (or add your own) to create your own words. You might mix roots with prefixes and suffixes to create new sciences or fields of study. Who knows, perhaps you will become a famous *sitcomologist.*

chron—time
garb—garbage
hydro—water
aster, astr—star

ist or *ologist*—one who studies a science
nomy—laws of a science or field
ology—the science or study of
phobia—fear of

_____

_____

Reading Artifacts

In "Tall City of Silent Stone," the author tells how archaeologist Hiram Bingham discovered the ruins of Machu Picchu. One of the challenges an archaeologist faces is learning how to "read" the clues that an ancient civilization leaves behind. To appreciate the challenge, play this simple game.

Directions: Pretend an archaeologist living in the distant future has made an important discovery—a teenager's room dated from the 1990s. In fact, the room is your room. But the archaeologist knows nothing of the living habits of a typical teenager today. The archaeologist must read the clues of your room. To do this, the archaeologist has started cataloging *artifacts*, or objects made by humans. Below is the beginning of the catalog. Complete the chart with observations and conclusions drawn from items that an archaeologist might find in your room.

Artifact	Observations	Conclusions
This round, green and silver container about 4½ inches tall looks like it might have been a drinking container.	Words written on the side read: carbonated water, high fructose corn syrup and/or sucrose, phosphoric acid, natural flavors.	The occupant of this dwelling must have liked sweet drinks.

OREGON, HO!

Prereading: Words in Context

Directions: "Oregon, Ho!" is an account of a woman who traveled the Oregon Trail in the 1850s. This activity will help you understand some of the words Mrs. Bailey uses to describe her adventure. Look over the definitions of the **bold-faced** words; then read the sentences in which they are used. Finally, use this information about the words to answer the questions below.

Word(s) in Context	Definition
1. "My mother's people were among the first settlers in America. They were **Quakers.**"	Many Quakers (members of the Religious Society of Friends) came to America for religious freedom.
2. "In…1851 a great wave of excitement, the **Western fever,** swept over all that part of the country."	People with Western fever were eager to move to unsettled parts of the western United States.
3. "Two days before we came to Chimney Rock the **cholera** struck us."	Cholera is a painful disease that causes cramps, vomiting, weakness, and diarrhea. It can be fatal.
4. "The modern mother would think twice before she let her 15-year-old daughter move out on a **tract** of timber, miles from any neighbor…"	A *tract* is a stretch or expanse of land.

1. In what part of the country—eastern, western, or central—did the author's grandmother probably live?

_____

2. Why did the author's family probably decide to go to Oregon?

_____

3. Name one danger that the pioneers faced on the Oregon Trail.

_____

4. Was Oregon fully settled when Mrs. Bailey got there? How do you know?

_____

OREGON, HO!

from Fred Lockley's *Conversations with Pioneer Women*
by Marilla R. Washburn Bailey

Reason to read: Interpret a firsthand account of the challenges faced by pioneers in Oregon.
As you read: This 1926 newspaper article reports a conversation with someone who actually traveled the Oregon Trail. As you read, look for details that help you understand the dangers and hardships her pioneer family faced.

"I was born in New York state, December 22, 1839. My maiden name was Marilla R. Washburn. My father, Alfred Washburn, and my mother, whose maiden name was Mary Jane Farrington, were born in New York state.

"My mother's people were among the first settlers in America. They were Quakers. Her grandfather and her father wore Quaker knee breeches with buckles at the knees. I remember very distinctly Grandfather always said 'thee' and 'thou.'

"Father was born in 1811 and Mother in 1812. There were 14 children of us—12 boys and 2 girls.

"We moved to Chicago in 1842. Father ran a transfer depot and a livery stable. He did draying and rented sleighs and carriages. I guess if some of our early-day neighbors in Chicago who died during the '40s could come back and take a look at Chicago as it is today they wouldn't know the place.

"In the fall and winter of 1851 a great wave of excitement, the Western fever, swept over all that part of the country. Nearly everybody was talking about the Willamette Valley, the Puget Sound country, or California. Father decided to go to Oregon. He made a contract to bring four families across the plains, he to furnish wagons, teams, and drivers for a stipulated amount. The contract he made was all right as far as it went, but it didn't go far enough, because the families he brought out were to pay him on arrival in Oregon, but it turned out that none of them had the money and, while all of them promised to pay later, none of them ever did.

"We started with five wagons. Father brought out some blooded [or purebred] mares. One of them was a fine Morgan mare. Two of our wagons were drawn by horses, the other three by oxen.

"Two days before we came to Chimney Rock the cholera struck us. Seven died in our train that night and four the next day. A young man in our wagon train named Hyde went out as a guard for the stock that night. When he left, after supper,

Oxen draw a covered wagon.
Denver Public Library

A wagon train crosses the prairie.
Library of Congress

he seemed perfectly well. When the guard was changed at midnight Mr. Wood brought his body back to the train. He had been taken with severe cramps and died within two hours.

"My brother and I both took the cholera. Mother gave us all the hot whiskey she could pour down us and put flannel cloths soaked in whiskey, as hot as we could bear them, on our stomachs. This cured us.

"Father was a veterinary surgeon. He had brought a lot of medicine for horses and cattle, and also the family medicine chest. My mother was a good practical nurse. In fact, she had to be, to raise 14 children.

"Shortly after my brother and I had the cholera we lay over half a day at Chimney Rock, and when we pulled on the next morning we had a new brother. Father and Mother had started across the plains with 12 children, so now, with our baby brother Melvin, there were 13. Another child was born after we came to Oregon.

"We crossed the Missouri River at St. Joe. There were 72 wagons and eight light buggies in our train. There were 170 men, women, and children. Captain Berry, the captain, took mountain fever and could no longer serve as captain, so my father was elected captain. Dr. Kellogg, one of the members of our train, always claimed that Captain Berry had yellow fever, but others thought he had mountain fever. Just after the Fourth of July some of the members of our train took smallpox and four died of it.

"My brother, Henry, just older than I, who was 14, was a fine horseman and an expert swimmer. When we reached the Snake River Father told Henry to take the stock across, where they could get better pasture. The horse Henry rode became frightened in the swift water and began faunching around and got into deep water. When my brother tried to get him back in the shallower water he reared up, threw Henry off his back, and kicked him in the head. We stayed there two days searching for my brother's body. Henry was drowned just above Salmon Falls. Mother wrote a notice and fastened it to a board beside the road, asking anyone who found Henry's body to

Pioneers stop to repair a wagon wheel.
Denver Public Library

"We ate buffalo meat and antelope. Some of the families ate sage-hens and jackrabbbits, but we kids didn't like them and would go hungry before we would eat them.

"When we got to The Dalles Father sold his blooded mares and his stock to the government. In those days there was a fort at The Dalles. Father left his five wagons there, intending to go back and get them later, but he never went back. We went from The Dalles to the Cascades on a flatboat. There we caught a small steamer for Vancouver. We stopped at Vancouver four days and then went to Portland, where we lived until 1854.

"My most vivid recollection of that first winter in Oregon is of the weeping skies and of Mother and me also weeping. I was homesick for my schoolmates in Chicago and I thought I would die. We knew no one in Portland. We had no use for Portland, nor for Oregon, and were convinced that we never would care for it. We stayed in Portland till 1854, when Father took up a donation land claim near what is now Kelso, Washington.

"I was married at Kelso shortly after my 15th birthday. My first baby, Amanda, was born in Fort Smith, in Cowlitz County, in 1856. The settlers had gathered in the fort there on account of the danger from the Indians. This was during the Indian War of 1855–56. I married John Black, who was born in Ireland and who had a farm near ours. We were married by a justice of the peace.

"In 1856 my parents moved to Olympia. When Amanda was 5 months old I put her into basket, hung it to the horn of my saddle and went to Olympia to visit my parents.

bury it and notify her. The next spring we got a letter from a man named Llewellyn, who had settled above Salem. He said he had found Henry's body and buried it. He sent Mother the things he had found in Henry's pockets. Just before leaving Chicago a chum of Henry's had given him a small horseshoe for good luck. Before we left home Mother wrote our names in indelible ink on strong pieces of cloth and sewed them inside our clothes. Mr. Llewellyn cut from Henry's jacket the label with his name on it and the little good luck horseshoe, and sent them to Mother.

"Just behind us was a train from Michigan. When the Indians attacked them they corralled and fought the Indians off, but four men in the wagon train were killed.

"We used to see a cloud of dust rising and Father would call out to get ready to divide the train. Soon we would hear a low roar, like the sound of surf, and then we would see a big herd of shaggy-haired buffaloes, their heads held low, running at a slow, lumbering trot to the river to drink. They wouldn't stop for anything, so we gave them the right of way. Several times we had to divide our train to let them through.

"There used to be a trading station named Monticello, where we traded. Later Seth Catlin started a store [at Freeport].

"I lived on our farm, five miles from Kelso, 25 years. All of my ten children were born on the farm. I had five girls and five boys. Four of my daughters and one son are still living.

"Forty-five years ago I moved to Portland. I ran a rooming house and took boarders on Yamhill Street, to support my children. Twenty-five years ago I went to Rossman, British Columbia, and for the next four years I worked as a practical nurse. There I met and married Orrin E. Bailey, a clerk in the hotel. We moved to Ferry County, in northern Washington. We used to trade at Midway, just across the line. Sixteen years ago we moved to St. Johns. My husband works in the woolen mills.

"I am 87 years old and as I look back to my girlhood I cannot help thinking how much more is done for the girls of today than was done for the girls of my day and generation. They have liberty that in our day was undreamed of. Sometimes I wonder if the girl of today is as self-reliant, self-sacrificing and as useful as girls were when I was a girl.

"I was married at 15, and was not only a good cook and housekeeper, but I knew how to take care of babies, from having cared for my brothers and sisters. I had ten babies of my own and never had help. I could paddle my canoe on the river or handle the oars in a rowboat as well as an Indian. When my husband was away I could rustle the meat on which we lived, for I could handle a revolver or rifle as well as most men. I have shot bears, deer, and all sorts of smaller game. I used to take my

revolver out and shoot the heads off grouse and pheasants. In fact, I became so expert with a revolver that at 50 to 100 feet I could beat most men.

"During the early days I lived in tents, in log pens, and in log cabins. The modern mother would think twice before she let her 15-year-old daughter move out on a tract of timber, miles away from any other settler, where she would have to kill the game for meat, cook over a fireplace, take care of the children, make soap and make clothes for the children. In those days we could not run into some handy store to get supplies.

"My first baby, Amanda, born at Fort Smith, Cowlitz County, in 1856, was married when she was 15. Her first child was a girl, whom she named Laura. Laura's first child was also a girl, who is now 13, and who, by the by, is my great-granddaughter. I hope I may live to see my great-granddaughter married and have a child, so I shall have a great-great-granddaughter."

Oregon Journal
March 3 & 4, 1926

Many pioneers lived in log cabins they built themselves.
Denver Public Library

OREGON, HO!

Identifying Important Details

First-hand accounts like Marilla Bailey's show what pioneer life was really like. But which of the many details she gives are important? Summarizing what you've just read is one way to find out.

Directions: Complete the summary below by filling in the blanks. Answer from memory or go back to the article.

1. **Family Background:** Marilla R. Washburn Bailey was born in New York in _____. Her family moved to _____ in 1842. There Mr. Washburn ran a transfer depot and _____ _____. When many people wanted to go west, he decided to move to _____.

2. **The Oregon Trail:** The family started out with five _____, drawn by horses and _____. Several members of the party died from _____. Marilla and her brother recovered because their mother was a skilled _____. When the party crossed the Missouri River, they had _____ wagons, _____ light buggies, and _____ people. The leader became ill, so the travelers elected _____ as the new captain. At Chimney Rock, Mrs. Washburn gave birth to her _____ th child. More members of the party died—this time from _____. Henry Washburn was _____ when his horse panicked crossing a river. His body was identified because _____ _____. The train behind the Washburns was attacked by _____. The wagon train often had to let herds of _____ through. The family's food included _____, _____, _____, and _____.

3. **Life in Oregon:** The Washburns ended their journey at _____. Marilla's first reaction to Oregon was _____, but they stayed. In 1854, the family claimed land near _____, Washington. Mrs. Bailey was married when she was _____ years old. Her first baby was born in a _____ where the settlers had gathered during an Indian war. After raising 10 children on John Black's farm, Mrs. Bailey moved to Portland. She took in _____ to support her children. She then became a _____ _____. After she married Orrin Bailey, she moved to St. Johns.

4. **Survival Skills:** Mrs. Bailey knew how to cook and keep house, take care of _____, and handle boats. She was also an expert _____ with a revolver. She lived in log _____ and cooked over a _____ instead of a stove. Since she had no _____, she had to rely on herself. She killed her own _____ and made her own _____ and clothes.

Analyzing an Interview

Reporter Fred Lockley chose to include only Mrs. Bailey's words in this article. He did not include any of the questions he asked. The activity below will help you determine the questions Mr. Lockley might have asked.

Directions: Match each question to Mrs. Bailey's answer.

Questions	Answers
_____ 1. Where were you born?	a. "The modern mother would think twice before she let her 15-year-old daughter move out on a tract of timber, miles away from any other settler."
_____ 2. What skills did you need to survive on the frontier?	b. "I was born in New York state, December 22, 1839…"
_____ 3. How is life different for girls today?	c. "I used to take my revolver out and shoot the heads off grouse and pheasants."
_____ 4. What do you look forward to?	d. "I was married at 15, and was not only a good cook and housekeeper, but I knew how to take care of babies…"
_____ 5. How did you develop your ability to handle a gun?	e. "I hope I may live to see my great-granddaughter married…"

Now read each answer below. Then make up the question that you think Mrs. Bailey might have been asked.

Question: _____

_____

Answer: "We ate buffalo meat and antelope. Some of the families ate sagehens and jackrabbbits, but we kids didn't like them and would go hungry before we would eat them."

Question: _____

_____

Answer: "In the fall and winter of 1851 a great wave of excitement, the Western fever, swept over all that part of the country. Nearly everybody was talking about the Willamette Valley, the Puget Sound country, or California. Father decided to go to Oregon."

ESCAPE FROM SLAVERY

by Smart Edward Walker

Reason to read: Learn how Smart Edward Walker escaped from slavery.

As you read: Like many slave narratives, this story begins with a description of what it was like to be a slave. The narrator then describes the dangerous journey to freedom. Find the two parts of this story.

During the years before the Civil War, many slaves escaped to freedom on the "Underground Railroad." This railroad had no trains or tracks; it was a network of hiding places for runaway slaves. This is the story of Smart Edward Walker's escape. Walker later became a wealthy businessman in Windsor, Canada.

I was born on the plantation of Hayden Nelson, in Kenton County, Kentucky. . . fifty-seven years ago. When I was fifteen years of age his son Thomas Nelson became my master. Thomas already owned the adjoining planta-tion, and other property, and was a tolerably rich man. When I was about four years of age I was put to work doing little chores around the house, and when I was ten I worked in the corn field with the grown-up slaves. . . .

But from the time I was a little boy it always ground my feelings to know that I had to work for another man. This feeling was not encouraged by my par-ents or the other slaves; it came from within me and grew with the years.

My owner was not a bad man, but at times he

Slave owners often advertised rewards for the return of their escaped slaves. This illustration was often used in these advertisements.

was flighty and unreasonable, and at other times he was very good and kind. I was a good judge of human nature, and even when I was a little boy I could read him like a book, and knew every twist and turn of his mind and char-acter. He also knew me pretty well, and never whipped me. He appreciated the fact that a good scolding hurt me as bad and made me as angry as if he gave me a whipping.

His son, Hayden, named after his grandfather, was two years younger than me, and we were great friends. He took a notion to play school master and teach the colored boys on the plantation to read and write. The boys came into the sitting room of the Nelson house and Hayden would teach them their letters. His father didn't like it, but he let his son have his way, under the belief that he would soon get tired of it, and that his scholars wouldn't have the patience to learn. The father was about right in the latter. All the colored boys dropped off one by one except me. I stuck to it, and learned so fast that the father couldn't stand it and made his son quit after about two weeks teaching. That was all the teaching I ever had.

. . . I worked on the farm every day, but from the time I was fifteen years old I was always studying how to run away. In 1855, when I was eighteen years old, I was just on the point of running away when my uncle and his wife and family ran away from a plantation near the Nelsons and were successful in reaching Canada. They ran away on a Saturday night and all the planters in that section knew it the next morning. My master heard of it too and shortly after breakfast had his horse saddled and rode away. I found out from a white friend of my master's that he had gone. . . to a negro trader.

I said nothing but I saw it all in a flash. He mistrusted me and had gone to the trader to sell me. On Sundays I generally went off the plantation, but that Sunday I stayed at home. I knew that if he sold me I would be carried down South to New Orleans and it would be almost impossible to escape from there to Canada. So I played my little game as well as I knew how. When my master came back he found me and his son and my brother pitching horseshoes in front of the house. . . . As he came near I didn't appear to see him, but I watched him out of the corner of my eye. There never was a happier boy than I appeared to be. I whooped and hollered and laughed, and as he passed in I thought I saw his countenance get less stern.

I found out afterwards that he had offered me

Library of Congress

The Fugitive Slave Law allowed slave-catchers to pursue escaped slaves and return them to their masters.

to the trader for a certain price, but the trader wanted me for less. So they agreed to talk about it again next day. The trader rode up next day and said he would take me at my master's price. But his offer was refused. My master wouldn't sell me, saying he had changed his mind. So you see I fooled him that time.

Early in 1858 my brother and I worked out a plan of escape. My brother was married to a girl that lived on a plantation four miles away and they had a little daughter. A colored man, who was also a slave, helped us. . . . He fixed matters with a white agent of the underground railroad in Cincinnati, who agreed to have a boat waiting for us on the river bank at a certain place in Covington [about ten miles from his plantation]. On a Wednesday night we started out to escape. My brother and I each took a horse from the barn and rode to where his wife was living. The colored friend bought a horse for himself. My brother sat his wife on his horse and I took his girl on mine and we left for Covington. When we got to within three miles of the town we dismounted. I and Moses turned our horses loose and the colored friend tied his to a tree in the woods. We set out on foot and got to Covington about midnight.

We had to be very cautious for a guard was supposed to be watching for runaways every night on the river bank. We had to cross a piece of quicksand about twelve feet across before we got to the bank. I didn't know what it was so I stood on it and handed my brother's wife and child across. Then my brother passed over and so did my friend. I turned to go too, when I found that I was stuck. I could not pull my feet out and I felt I was sinking. I didn't dare call out as I was afraid the guard would catch us.

But when my brother went to the boat he found that I had not followed so he came back and found me. It was rather hard work, but he pulled me out. We all got in the small boat and the white agent rowed us across to Cincinnati. We were taken to the house of a colored family and stayed there about a week and then left for Canada. My brother and his family and myself rode in one buggy with a white driver. The other buggy was occupied by three fugitives—one woman and two men—and a white man as driver. We travelled at night and slept in farmer's houses by day, until we reached Bellefontaine,[2] Ohio and then took the train for Sandusky.[3] There we took the boat for Detroit, and came across on the ferryboat, landing here on April 20, 1858.

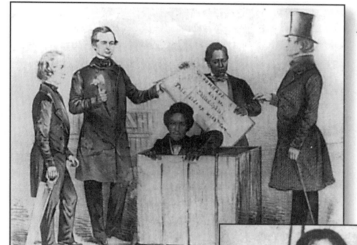

Henry "Box" Brown escaped from slavery by having himself sealed inside a box and mailed to freedom. Other slaves then followed Brown's example.

Slaves who were captured after attempting to escape were often restrained. This Louisiana slave wears a choker and chains.
Library of Congress

1 *countenance:* outward look or appearance
2 Bellefontaine is a small town in west-central Ohio.
3 Sandusky is an Ohio town on Lake Erie.

Reading for Answers

Directions: Choose the sentence from Walker's story that best answers each question below.

1. Why did Walker want to be free?

   Ⓐ "…When I was ten I worked in the cornfield with the grown-up slaves…."

   Ⓑ "From the time I was a little boy it always ground my feelings to know that I had to work for another man."

2. How did Walker learn to read?

   Ⓐ "My owner…[at times] was very good and kind."

   Ⓑ "[My master's son] took a notion to play school master."

3. What conclusion did Walker draw when his master visited the slave trader?

   Ⓐ "He mistrusted me and had gone to the trader to sell me."

   Ⓑ "All the planters in that section knew [of his uncle's escape]."

4. How did Walker fool his master?

   Ⓐ "…From the time I was fifteen years old I was always studying how to run away."

   Ⓑ "There never was a happier boy than I appeared to be."

5. What dangers did Walker face when he escaped?

   Ⓐ "A colored man…fixed matters with a white agent of the underground railroad."

   Ⓑ "…A guard was supposed to be watching for runaways every night on the riverbank. We had to cross a piece of quicksand…"

Tracing a Journey to Freedom

Directions: Use information from Walker's story to trace his journey on the map on page 119. Your knowledge of how the piece is organized will help you find the place names you need.

1. Where did Walker's journey begin? _____

    Quote the sentence or state it in your own words. _____

    _____

2. Where did Smart Edward and his relatives meet the first agent of the Underground Railroad? _____

    Quote the sentence or state it in your own words. _____

    _____

3. Where did the Walkers stay before they left for Canada? _____

    Quote the sentence or state it in your own words. _____

    _____

4. What town did the Walkers travel to at night? _____

    Quote the sentence or state it in your own words. _____

    _____

5. Where did they catch the boat for Detroit? _____

    Quote the sentence or state it in your own words. _____

    _____

6. In what country did their journey end? _____

    Quote the sentence or state it in your own words. _____

    _____

Routes on the Underground Railroad

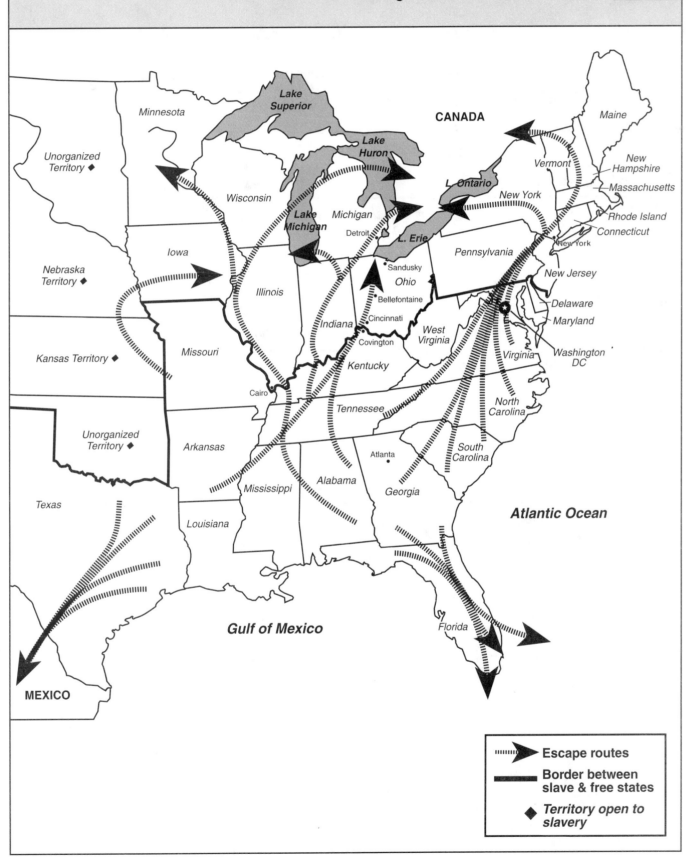

Lake Superior

CANADA

Maine

Minnesota

Lake Huron

Vermont

New Hampshire

Massachusetts

Unorganized Territory ◆

Wisconsin

L. Ontario

New York

Rhode Island

Connecticut

Michigan

Lake Michigan

New York

Iowa

Detroit

L. Erie

Pennsylvania

Nebraska Territory ◆

Sandusky

Ohio

New Jersey

Delaware

Illinois

Bellefontaine

Maryland

Cincinnati

West Virginia

Washington DC

Kansas Territory ◆

Missouri

Covington

Indiana

Kentucky

Virginia

Cairo

Tennessee

North Carolina

Unorganized Territory ◆

Arkansas

Atlanta

South Carolina

Texas

Alabama

Georgia

Atlantic Ocean

Mississippi

Louisiana

Florida

Gulf of Mexico

MEXICO

Legend

🢒 Escape routes

▬▬ Border between slave & free states

◆ Territory open to slavery

Synthesizing Information

The answers to these questions are not directly stated in Walker's story. However, you can answer them by *synthesizing*, or combining, information from his account and the map on page 119. The example below shows how one reader combined information to answer the first question.

Directions: Read the example, then complete the chart.

Question	Answer
1. Why do you think so many slaves chose to follow these routes instead of finding their own path to freedom?	*It seems that the runaways could have just headed north. But wait…Walker mentioned having to avoid a guard. And in Ohio, they traveled at night to avoid being caught. So runaways had a better chance of escaping if someone helped them hide. Also, Walker's master didn't want his slaves to learn to read. But the map shows that most slaves had a long journey north. So they would have had a hard time following a map to freedom.*
2. Why did slaves escaping from Missouri go through Kansas and Nebraska?	
3. Why do you think runaway slaves living in Florida went south instead of north?	
4. Explain why slaves escaping from Illinois might have crossed Lake Huron.	

Prereading: Reading Illustrations

The illustrations in social studies books aren't there just for observation. Pictures, maps, and charts contain information. In fact, you can "read" an illustration just as you read words. Here's how.

First, *scan* the illustration—take a quick look at it to see what it's about. Then look at what attracts your attention most. You might move on to other details of the picture. You should also read the title, the caption, or other information around the picture and then look at the picture again.

Directions: "Read" the picture in the left-hand column. Then write your responses to the questions in the right-hand column. You'll probably find it helpful to move back and forth between the picture and the questions.

Egyptians believed that baskets of grain and animals shown in tomb paintings like this one would nourish a person's soul, or ka, throughout eternity.

What do I notice first about this artwork?

What other things do I notice?

What questions do I have about this artwork?

What do I know about the time and place in which it was created?

What information have I gotten from this artwork?

ART FOR THE AFTERLIFE

by Mary Lindeen

Reason to read: Find out what the ancient Egyptians' views of death reveal about their way of life.
As you read: Use the information in this article to interpret the painting on page 123. You'll probably find it easiest to move back and forth between the picture and this article.

The Egyptians believed the soul or spirit lived on after death in a pleasant after-life. It could do all the things the person had done on earth—eat, drink, sing, and move about. But the soul needed to return to its body from time to time. So the Egyptians invented the process of making mummies. Only important people could afford to be mummified.

Pharoahs were buried with everything needed for the afterlife. Jewelry, clothes, cosmetics, furniture, games, chariots—even ships—have been found in their tombs. Cats were sacred to the Egyptians, and mummi-fied pets were often buried with their rich owners.

Paintings decorate the walls of many tombs. These wall paintings often show scenes from the lives of those buried in the tombs. They depict their food, work, and favorite possessions. These pictures repre-sent what the owner of the tomb hoped to do in the afterlife. Once the tombs were sealed, the Egyptians believed that the people and objects in the paintings became real.

Tomb paintings include several common elements. Each element is carefully drawn, since people and objects were believed to come to life as they were painted. For example, the contents of containers are piled on top so the contents can be seen. Otherwise, the person buried in the tomb would not be able to use what was in the container.

Characteristics of Egyptian Art

- Titles and descriptions are written in hieroglyphics.

- Scenes are split horizontally. The action begins in the bottom right scene.

- Human figures have perfect bodies and youthful beauty. (They could then come back to life with no defects.)

- Drawings are detailed, with the contents of baskets and other containers clearly shown. (The dead would have everything they needed.)

- The perspective, or viewpoint, is unusual.

  —People are drawn so as little of the body as possible is hidden. The head faces sideways. The eye and shoulders face forward. Everything from the waist down faces sideways again. One leg and one foot are usually in front of the other. (The entire body is shown so that its owner would be whole in the afterlife.)

  —People hold objects with their fingers above or below but never around them. (The object will then be whole in the afterlife.)

  —Important people are larger than other figures.

  —Peasants and animals are drawn more realistically. (They were less important, so it did not matter how they looked when they came to life.)

- The Nile is drawn as a large band of color with fish in it.

- The artist's identity is not known. (Artists were considered officials of the state who performed a particular service, like carpenters.)

Harvest Tomb Painting

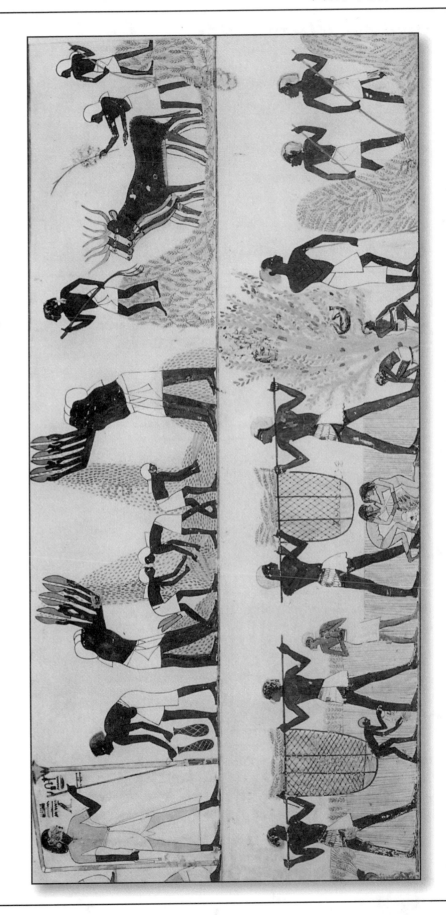

This Egyptian tomb painting depicts the many steps of a wheat harvest. The action begins in the lower right corner, with farmers raising grain near the banks of the Nile. Ultimately, laborers deliver an offering of grain to a god in the upper left corner. The god is holding a staff of prosperity. Perhaps the people making the offering are slaves, for only the rich owned oxen such as those shown in the upper right. Harvest offerings such as this one are frequently shown in tomb paintings.

ART FOR THE AFTERLIFE

Interpreting an Illustration

Directions: Complete the sentences below. You may need to write several additional sentences.

The Harvest Tomb Painting on page 123 shows…

Its style and subject matter are typical of Egyptian art in these ways.

The painting is untypical because…

Some questions I was able to answer about this painting are…

From studying this painting, I learned that the Egyptians…

Creating Callouts

Important parts of an illustration are often labeled with *callouts.* Lines connect the callout to what it labels.

Directions: Create callouts for the parts of the picture below.

Detail from Harvest Painting

1. _____

2. _____

3. _____

4. _____

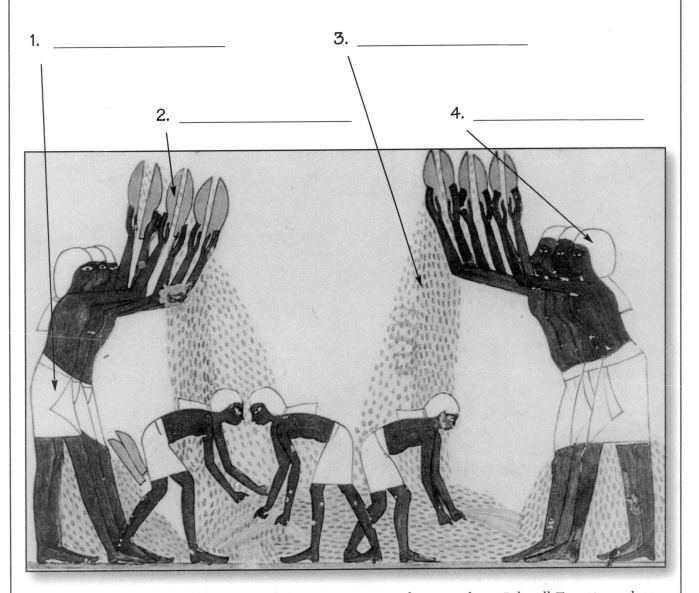

In this detail from the tomb painting, farmers use sieves to harvest wheat. Like all Egyptians, these farmers wear clothing made of linen. Men generally wore short white kilts and women wore longer, closer fitting dresses. To shield themselves from the blazing Egyptian sun, the men pictured here also wear linen head scarves. Linen is made from the flax plant which grows along the Nile.

READING FOR INFORMATION SELF-CHECK

When I come to a word I don't know, I

_____ see if I can guess the meaning from the words around it.

_____ ask someone or look it up.

_____ sound it out.

_____ _____

When a whole sentence doesn't make sense, I

_____ read it again.

_____ see if anything in the paragraph helps me figure it out.

_____ sound out the hardest words.

_____ _____

Before I start to read, I think about

_____ why I'm reading this selection.

_____ what I want to learn.

_____ what I might need to remember.

_____ _____

As I read for information, I

_____ first look the piece over to get an idea of what it's about.

_____ ask myself questions about what I'm reading.

_____ take notes on things I need to remember.

_____ _____

As I read biographies, I

_____ recall what I already know about this person or the time period.

_____ look for details that make this person come alive.

_____ try to find things I have in common with the subject of the biography.

_____ _____

Reading for Information Self-Check *continued*

When I read something about history, I

_____ expect that I might have to adapt to a writing style that's different from what I'm used to.

_____ look for clues about the time at which the piece was written.

_____ try to connect new information to what I already know.

_____ _____

When I read something about science or technology, I

_____ try to figure out how the writer organized the piece.

_____ make sure I know what each scientific or technical word means.

_____ try to connect new information to what I already know.

_____ _____

After I read, I think about

_____ the most important thing I learned.

_____ how what I learned relates to what I already know.

_____ whether I agree or disagree with the author.

_____ _____

Each time you complete this self-check, compare your answers to your answers the last time you completed it. Then answer these questions.

What is the most important thing you learned from your work with reading skills and strategies?

_____

_____

Describe a time when you used one of these skills or strategies in another class.

_____

_____

What tips would you give another student who was having trouble reading in social studies?

_____

_____

What tips would you give another student who was having trouble reading in science?

_____

_____

Text Acknowledgments

"Charles," reprinted from *The Lottery,* copyright © 1948 by Shirley Jackson. Reprinted by permission of Farrar, Straus & Giroux, Inc.

"Priscilla and the Wimps" by Richard Peck, copyright © 1984 by Richard Peck. From *Sixteen: Short Stories* by Donald R. Gallo, ed. Used by permission of Dell Books, a division of Bantam Doubleday Dell Publishing Group, Inc.

"The No-Guitar Blues" by Gary Soto. From *Baseball in April and Other Stories,* copyright © 1990 by Gary Soto. Reprinted with permission of Harcourt Brace & Company.

"Foul Shot" by Edwin Hoey. Special permission granted from READ Magazine and published by Weekly Reader Corporation. Copyright © renewed 1989, 1962 by Weekly Reader Corporation. All rights reserved.

"The Sea" from *The Wandering Moon* by James Reeves. Copyright © 1950 by James Reeves. Reprinted with permission of William Heinemann Limited.

"Catalogue" by Rosalie Moore. Reprinted by permission; © 1940 The New Yorker Magazine, Inc.

"Attack of the Gator" reprinted from *True Fright: Trapped Beneath the Ice! and Other True Stories Scarier than Fiction* by Ted Pederson. Copyright © 1996 by Tor Books. Reprinted with permission.

"A Suspicious Package" from *Bomb Squads and SWAT Teams* by Jean Dick. Copyright © 1988 by Crestwood House Publishers. Reprinted with permission of Silver Burnett Ginn Publishing.

"My Four-Legged Partner in Healing" reprinted from *Love, Miracles and Animal Healing* by Allen M. Schoen, DVM, MS and Pam Proctor. Copyright © 1995 by Allen M. Schoen, DVM, MS and Pam Proctor. Reprinted with permission of Simon & Schuster Publishers.

"Self-Defense" excerpt from *Stories from My Life* by Cassandra Walker, copyright © 1997. Used with permission from Free Spirit Publishing Inc., Minneapolis, MN; (800) 735-7323. ALL RIGHTS RESERVED.

"Branch Rickey Signs Jackie Robinson" from: *Jackie Robinson and the Breaking of the Color Barrier* by Russell Shorto, Copyright © 1991 by Russell Shorto and reprinted by permission of the Millbrook Press, Inc.

"All in a Day's Work" from *All in a Day's Work* by Neil Johnson. Copyright © 1989 by Neil Johnson. By permission of Little, Brown and Company.

"Tall City of Silent Stone" from *Lost Cities* by Joyce Goldenstern. Copyright © 1996 by Joyce Goldenstern. Reprinted with permission of Enslow Publishers, Inc.

"Oregon, Ho!" from *Conversations with Pioneer Women* by Fred Lockley. Copyright © 1981 by Fred Lockley. Reprinted with permission of Rainy Day Press, Inc.